OPERATION JUST CAUSE

The Planning and Execution of Joint Operations in Panama

February 1988 – January 1990

Ronald H. Cole

Joint History Office
Office of the Chairman of the Joint Chiefs of Staff
Washington, D.C. 1995

FOREWORD

Written shortly after the completion of Operation JUST CAUSE, this monograph traces the involvement of the Chairman of the Joint Chiefs of Staff and the Joint Staff in planning and directing combat operations in Panama. The study begins with the initial development of contingency plans in February 1988 and concludes with General Manuel Noriega's surrender to U.S. officials on 3 January 1990. Relying primarily upon Joint Staff files and interviews with key participants, the author, Dr. Ronald Cole, provides an account of the parts played by the Chairman of the Joint Chiefs of Staff, the Joint Staff, and the Commander in Chief of U.S. Southern Command in planning for operations in Panama and their roles in the combat operations that followed.

In accomplishing his task, Dr. Cole received valuable assistance from a large number of the key participants and members of the Joint Staff; their contributions are noted in the endnotes. The final manuscript was reviewed by Mr. Willard J. Webb and Dr. Walter S. Poole, edited by Ms. Penny Norman and typed by Ms. Helga Echols.

This monograph was reviewed for declassification by the appropriate U.S. government departments and agencies and cleared for release. Although the text has been declassified, some of the cited sources remain classified. The volume is an official publication of the Office of the Chairman of the Joint Chiefs of Staff, but the views expressed are those of the author and do not necessarily represent the official position of the Chairman or of the Joint Chiefs of Staff.

DAVID A. ARMSTRONG
Director for Joint History

Washington, D.C.
November 1995

CONTENTS

OVERVIEW

In the summer and fall of 1989, while American attention focused on events in Eastern Europe which heralded the end of the Cold War, developments in Panama raised the possibility of combat much closer to home. Operations in Panama would test the changes to the U.S. military command system brought about by the Goldwater-Nichols Defense Reorganization Act of 1986. Panama would also try the team at the head of that system—President George H. W. Bush, Secretary of Defense Richard B. Cheney, and the new Chairman of the Joint Chiefs of Staff (CJCS), General Colin L. Powell, U.S. Army. Strengthened by personal relationships formed during earlier administrations, this team would, in a large measure, determine the operational success of the Goldwater-Nichols reforms.

Questions about the effectiveness of the Joint Chiefs of Staff (JCS) and the system of unified commands had been raised at intervals since the Vietnam War. In 1982 the retiring Chairman, General David C. Jones, U.S. Air Force, proposed increasing the authority of the Chairman and the commanders in chief (CINCs) of the unified commands and strengthening the joint staffs supporting them. Fueled by reported shortcomings in service cooperation and interoperability during the 1983 invasion of Grenada and by the role of a cumbersome chain of command in the deaths of 241 U.S. Marines in a terrorist bombing in Beirut, criticism of the Joint Chiefs of Staff system prompted lengthy congressional deliberations and eventual enactment of the changes Jones had proposed.

Widely viewed as the most significant defense legislation since the National Security Act of 1947, Goldwater-Nichols sought to streamline the command and control of U.S. military forces engaged in contingency operations. After designating the CJCS as the President's principal military advisor, the Act made the Chairman specifically responsible for the preparation and review of contingency plans—a function he performed in conjunction with the CINCs. It further allowed the President to direct that communications between the National Command Authorities and the commanders of the unified commands be transmitted through the Chairman. The CINCs were, in turn, given full combatant command authority over their service components allowing them to control the organization and employment of these forces. Operation JUST CAUSE would demonstrate the effect of these changes.

In 1988, as relations with Panama deteriorated, the commander of U.S. Southern Command (SOUTHCOM), General Frederick F. Woerner, Jr., U.S. Army, had developed a strategy which gradually increased the strength of U.S. forces in Panama to deter the dictator, General Manuel

Noriega, from attacking U.S. citizens or interfering with the Panama Canal. If deterrence failed, Woerner planned to bring in additional forces from the United States over a three-week period before taking action against Noriega. But after Noriega overturned the results of the Panamanian election of May 1989, President Bush lost patience with General Woerner's approach and replaced him with General Maxwell R. Thurman, U.S. Army. Aggressive by nature, Thurman modified the BLUE SPOON plan to accommodate a major shift in the strategy for dealing with Noriega. Accelerating the buildup of U.S. forces in Panama, Thurman also shortened the timetable for the deployment of additional forces from the U.S. to three days. Hoping to take Noriega by surprise, General Thurman intended to overwhelm the dictator's forces before they could organize effective resistance or take U.S. citizens hostage.

Thurman took advantage of the CINC's power under Goldwater-Nichols to select Lieutenant General Carl W. Stiner, U.S. Army, the Commander of the XVIIIth Airborne Corps, to command a joint task force of 22,000 soldiers, 3,400 airmen, 900 Marines, and 700 sailors. General Powell approved Thurman's action. The result was a force with unity of command and good interoperability which would rapidly achieve its operational objectives.

In late 1989 relations with Panama grew sharply worse. On 15 December 1989, the National Assembly passed a resolution that a state of war existed with the United States, and Noriega named himself the Maximum Leader. Violence followed the next evening when a Panamanian soldier shot three American officers; one, First Lieutenant Robert Paz, U.S. Marine Corps, died of his wounds. Witnesses to the incident, a U.S. naval officer and his wife, were assaulted by Panamanian Defense Force (PDF) soldiers while in police custody. On 17 December, after a review of these events and a briefing on BLUE SPOON, President Bush decided to act. Operation JUST CAUSE began shortly before 0100 on 20 December with special operations forces attacking key installations in Panama.

In the early hours of 20 December, conventional task forces seized additional key points and the land approaches to Panama City. Task Force BAYONET then entered the city, secured the U.S. embassy and captured the PDF headquarters, *La Comandancia*, after a three- hour fight. With the *Comandancia* in U.S. hands and Noriega in hiding, centralized control of the PDF collapsed. However, fighting would flare sporadically for some time as U.S. forces overcame pockets of resistance.

As General Stiner's force attained its objectives, General Powell became more directly involved in military operations due to the growing importance of the political aspects of JUST CAUSE. He did so to ensure that actions in Panama meshed with the administration's political and diplomatic goals. During the first two days of the operation, Powell told Thurman to accelerate the drive to liberate the Marriott Hotel which held Americans who could become hostages. Powell also encouraged Thurman to move quickly to install the legally-elected government of Panama in office to discredit claims that Noriega still governed or that U.S. military rule was imminent.

After Noriega fled to the papal *Nunciatura*, U.S. troops played loud rock music outside the residence. When the Vatican and the diplomatic community complained to President Bush about this harassment, the Chairman ordered Thurman to stop the noise. Powell urged Thurman to have members of the new Panamanian government appeal directly to church officials in Panama and Rome for help in dislodging Noriega from the *Nunciatura*.

The operational success of JUST CAUSE rewarded efforts by Congress and the Bush administration to avoid repeating the mistakes of Lebanon and Grenada. The determination of President Bush and the enhanced authority of the Chairman and CINC combined to provide specific, readily attainable objectives and responsive and effective command and control while giving the tactical commander considerable operational freedom. However, when shortcomings in prior planning and mistakes by local commanders embarrassed the administration, General Powell acted to ensure the political success of the operation.

Chapter 1

Background of the Crisis

Before Noriega

Panama is an isthmus nearly four hundred miles long and fifty miles wide that connects Central America to the South American continent. About the size of South Carolina, Panama contains nearly 2.3 million Spanish-speaking people, most of mixed Spanish and Indian blood. Once a part of the Spanish colony that later became Colombia, Panama won its independence in 1903. That year, in the Hay-Bunau-Varilla Treaty, the new nation agreed to let the United States build a canal across the narrow part of the isthmus to link the Atlantic and the Pacific Oceans. In 1914 the United States completed the project within a U.S.-controlled "Canal Zone" extending five miles on either side of the 52-mile long waterway.

For more than six decades the Panama Canal played a pivotal role in U.S. strategic and commercial undertakings. In the age of transcontinental airplanes and intercontinental missiles, however, the importance of the Canal to the U.S. diminished. Meanwhile, Panamanian nationalists increasingly resented the U.S. presence in their country. Eventually, U.S.-Panamanian negotiations led to an agreement whereby the United States promised to cede control of the Canal to Panama by the year 2000. In ratifying this treaty, the U.S. Senate inserted a proviso that permitted the United States to continue to defend the Panama Canal after 1999 if any interruption in the operation of the waterway occurred. The senators noted, however, that this proviso should not be interpreted as giving the United States the right to intervene in Panama's internal affairs or otherwise infringe upon that country's sovereignty.

In the decade following treaty ratification, the Joint Chiefs of Staff continued to view the Panama Canal as of great strategic value. During a conflict in Western Europe or the Middle East, possession of the Canal would speed the movement of U.S. naval vessels from the Pacific to the Atlantic. In the hands of a government opposed to the United States, the JCS believed that Panama could be used as a wartime base by the Soviet Union or one of its client states, such as Cuba, to attack U.S. maritime operations or, in peacetime, to support left-wing insurgencies in Central America and drug trafficking with the United States.[1]

The Rise of Noriega

Manuel Antonio Noriega rose to power as an intelligence officer in the service of the dictator, Brigadier General Omar Torrijos. After the death of Torrijos in 1983, Noriega took over the Panama Defense Force (PDF), an organization that included the armed forces, police, customs and investigative services of Panama. Noriega continued his practice of cultivating friends and patrons within the U.S. intelligence community and clients within the Medellín drug cartel of Colombia. In 1985 the National Security Adviser to President Ronald W. Reagan, Vice Admiral John M. Poindexter, U.S. Navy, and the Assistant Secretary of State for Inter-American Affairs, Elliott Abrams, warned Noriega of U.S. concern over his monopoly of power and involvement in the drug trade.

The first public confrontation between Noriega and the United States took place in June 1987. A former chief of staff in the PDF, Colonel Roberto Díaz-Herrera, accused his old master of complicity in the death of Torrijos, electoral fraud, and the 1985 murder of the leader of Noriega's political opposition, Hugo Spadafora. During the anti-Noriega demonstrations that ensued, Noriega's riot police suppressed the unarmed demonstrators. The U.S. Senate promptly passed a resolution calling for the dictator to step down. A pro-Noriega mob attacked the U.S. embassy, and the State Department cut off economic and military aid to Panama. On 5 February 1988, federal grand juries in Miami and Tampa, Florida, indicted Noriega and his key henchmen on numerous counts of involvement in drug trafficking. Noriega demonstrated his defiance by replacing the nominal chief of state, President Eric Arturo Delvalle, with a Noriega crony, Manuel Solis Palma. Throughout 1988 and 1989, Noriega supported a campaign of harassing U.S. citizens in Panama and hindered full U.S. implementation of its rights under the 1977 Panama Canal treaties.[2]

In 1988 and 1989 Noriega turned to Cuba, Nicaragua, and Libya for economic and military assistance. Cuba and Nicaragua funneled Communist bloc weapons and instructors to Panama and helped Noriega to develop civilian defense committees, the so-called Dignity Battalions, for intelligence collection and population control. Libya contributed $20 million in 1989 in return for Noriega's permission to use Panama as a base to coordinate the activities of terrorist and insurgent groups throughout Latin America.[3]

Even before the full impact of Cuban and Nicaraguan aid, the PDF contained 19 companies and 6 platoons numbering some 14,000 men, of whom at least 4,000 were well-trained and equipped for combat; equipment included 29 armored personnel carriers, 12 patrol craft, and 28 light transport aircraft. The PDF was expected to strongly defend its headquarters, *La Comandancia*, in Panama City, as well as its bases at Fort Amador, Rio Hato, and the Torrijos-Tucumen International Airport. In addition, PDF forces had the capability to conduct sabotage and stand-off attacks against the Canal and U.S. military installations such as Quarry Heights, Fort Clayton, Howard Air Force Base, Albrook Air Force Base, and the U.S. naval station at Rodman. Noriega's forces could retreat into the mountains and jungles of the interior and conduct prolonged guerrilla warfare.[4]

Contingency Planning Begins, February–November 1988

After the U.S. federal indictments, the Joint Chiefs of Staff directed General Frederick F. Woerner, Jr., U.S. Army, the Commander in Chief of U.S. Southern Command (USCINCS0), to revise contingency plans intended to protect U.S. lives and property, to keep open the Canal, to conduct noncombatant evacuation operations in peaceful or hostile environments, and to develop a plan to assist any government that might replace the Noriega regime. General Woerner and his director of operations, Brigadier General Marc A. Cisneros, U.S. Army (SOUTHCOM J-3), began work on a series of contingency plans collectively known as ELABORATE MAZE. Working with them was Major General Bernard Loeffke, commander of the U.S. Army South (USARSO), who would execute the plans as Commander, Joint Task Force Panama.[5]

Based upon guidance from the Joint Chiefs of Staff, Woerner's early contingency plans envisioned a massive buildup of forces within U.S. bases in Panama that would either intimidate the PDF leaders under Noriega and cause them to overthrow him or, failing that, provide a force capable of invading Panamanian territory and overthrowing the PDF. President Reagan, Secretary of Defense Frank C. Carlucci, Chairman of the Joint Chiefs of Staff Admiral William J. Crowe, Jr., and General Woerner favored the mass approach over a surprise strategy, where forces from the United States would in concert with special operations forces and General Woerner's troops conduct a sudden attack against Noriega and the PDF. At that time, concern was expressed that failure to capture Noriega soon after the initial assault might allow him to flee to the hills and organize guerrilla warfare. He might also order the abduction or killing of a number of the nearly thirty-five thousand U.S. citizens residing in Panama.

As Noriega ignored U.S. signals and became increasingly brutal during the next year, emphasis shifted toward a plan that embodied elements of both strategies. On 16 March 1988, a faction of the

Panama Defense Force staged a coup attempt at *La Comandancia*. Noriega suppressed the effort and purged the PDF of those whose loyalty he considered lukewarm. He also declared a state of national emergency, cracked down on political opposition, and stepped up anti-U.S. harassment, chiefly through severe travel restrictions, searches, and roadblocks.

Chairman Crowe asked General Woerner to break down ELABORATE MAZE into four separate operation orders to facilitate execution. General Woerner's staff named the four operation orders collectively PRAYER BOOK. The first operation order, KLONDIKE KEY, covered noncombatant evacuation operations escorting U.S. citizens located throughout Panama to assembly areas in Panama City and Colón for evacuation to the United States.

The second operation order, POST TIME, planned for the employment of the 193d Infantry Brigade in Panama and forces deploying from the continental United States and the U.S. Atlantic Command, to defend U.S. citizens, U.S. installations, and the Panama Canal. The deploying forces would include a brigade from the 7th Infantry Division (Light), the 6th Marine Expeditionary Brigade, one mechanized infantry battalion, and a carrier battle group. Incorporated into the computerized force deployment list, called Time-Phased Force and Deployment Data (TPFDD), these forces would constitute the bulk of the force to be used for implementing the other two operation orders in the PRAYER BOOK series, BLUE SPOON and BLIND LOGIC.[6]

BLUE SPOON called for a joint offensive operation to defeat and dismantle the Panama Defense Force while protecting U.S. lives, U.S. property, and the Canal. As conceived by General Woerner and his staff, BLUE SPOON would begin with operations lasting up to eight days, conducted by the nearly twelve thousand troops already in Panama, who would then be joined, over a two-week period, by approximately ten thousand troops from the United States. A carrier battle group would interdict air and sea routes to Cuba and provide close air support while an amphibious task force would provide additional ground troops. In addition to U.S.-based forces listed for POST TIME, the SOUTHCOM commander would employ a joint task force of special operations forces from the U.S. Special Operations Command (SOCOM) for operations against the PDF leadership, command and control facilities, and airfields. The special operations forces would also be tasked with the rescue of hostages, the conduct of reconnaissance in support of Joint Task Force Panama, and the location and seizure of Manuel Noriega.

The SOUTHCOM commander would exercise overall command of BLUE SPOON with U.S. Atlantic Command (LANTCOM), U.S. Transportation Command (TRANSCOM), Strategic Air Command (SAC),

U.S. Pacific Command (PACOM), and U.S. Forces Command (FORSCOM) in support. SOUTHCOM would also be the tactical coordinating command with the Commander of Joint Task Force Panama and the Commander of the Joint Special Operations Task Force conducting simultaneous, but separate, operations. The command and control arrangement for BLUE SPOON posed one other difficulty: the senior major general commanding the 7th Infantry Division (L) would serve under a junior major general commanding Joint Task Force Panama.[7]

Once the initial assaults of BLUE SPOON had been completed, the joint task force could begin civil-military operations under the fourth operation order in the PRAYER BOOK series, BLIND LOGIC. Except for the carrier battle group, BLIND LOGIC would use the forces for POST TIME and BLUE SPOON with the addition of a civil affairs brigade. Planners from SOUTHCOM envisioned execution of BLIND LOGIC in three phases. During the immediate phase, civil affairs units would support ongoing combat actions and civilian efforts to reestablish public safety and public health measures. During the sustained phase, BLIND LOGIC operations would focus on restoring other essential services and transferring control over them to Panamanian and U.S. civilians. In the long range phase, U.S. civil affairs troops would work with the new Panamanian government to reconstruct the PDF, reducing its size and powers and institutionalizing its loyalty to civilian authority and democratic government.[8]

From April 1988 until the summer of 1989 Lieutenant General Thomas W. Kelly, U.S. Army, the Director of Operations on the Joint Staff (J-3), disagreed with the SOUTHCOM J-3, Brigadier General Cisneros, on the chain of command to execute BLUE SPOON. The disagreement began when General Cisneros contended that Major General Loeffke's Joint Task Force Panama (JTFPM) should be the principal planning and operational headquarters. General Kelly and his staff argued that General Loeffke's JTFPM was only adequate to command the forces already in Panama. Once additional brigades from the U.S. deployed, a corps commander would be needed to command and control JTFPM, the 7th Infantry Division (L), and the Joint Special Operations Task Force. In General Kelly's view, the XVIIIth Airborne Corps had the staff and the rapid deployment capability needed to plan and execute BLUE SPOON.[9]

General Woerner resolved the dispute temporarily during the summer of 1988. His staff had recently been augmented with at least thirteen personnel, and USCINCSO had offered him special operations planners as well. With such expertise and the experience his staff had with Noriega and the PDF, Woerner believed that SOUTHCOM was fully qualified to serve as the warfighting headquarters for BLUE SPOON.

However, he recognized that if it became necessary to bolster JTFPM forces with brigades from the United States, a corps headquarters would be needed to run the operation. Thus, on 5 July 1988, General Woerner requested that Admiral Crowe include a corps headquarters in the force list for BLUE SPOON, that is; within the POST TIME TPFDD. In General Woerner's mind, the corps headquarters would not become operational until after the operation began. Admiral Crowe approved the CINC's request on 19 October and directed the Commander in Chief of Forces Command, General Joseph T. Palastra, Jr., U.S. Army, to revise the TPFDD accordingly. Nine days later, General Palastra authorized the commander of the XVIIIth Airborne Corps to establish liaison with SOUTHCOM.[10]

According to General Woerner, the XVIIIth Airborne Corps' assumption of tactical command and control would occur only after the execution of BLUE SPOON had begun, when he found it necessary to deploy all U.S.-based forces listed in the TPFDD of POST TIME. For this reason, the commander of the XVIIIth Airborne Corps initially delegated planning responsibility back to JTFPM headquarters. Throughout the period from July 1988 to summer 1989, however, the corps commander monitored the development of JTFPM planning for the operation.[11]

Unhappy with a command arrangement he believed incremental and disjointed, Lieutenant General Kelly met with the J-3s from SOUTHCOM and FORSCOM on 8 November 1988. They discussed two questions: Should the corps headquarters deploy in increments or completely? And should it deploy soon after execution had begun, or later, after all combat forces had deployed? General Kelly tried without success to convince SOUTHCOM J-3 to deploy the corps headquarters as a complete package before all combat forces had deployed. Admiral Crowe apparently sympathized with Kelly's preference, but did not overrule SOUTHCOM at that time.[12]

Nullifying the May 1989 Elections; Operation NIMROD DANCER

On 7 May 1989, Panamanians elected candidates of the anti-Noriega coalition. Leading the opposition, Guillermo Endara defeated Noriega's candidate for president, Carlos Duque, by a three to one margin. Endara's vice presidential running mates, Ricardo Arias Calderón and Guillermo Ford, did equally well. Despite the presence of observers from the Catholic Church and former President Jimmy Carter, Noriega's goon squads, notably members of the Dignity Battalions, tried to coerce the voters into electing Noriega's candidates. On 10 May, Noriega attributed the election results to foreign interference, annulled them, and sanctioned violence against the winners. After being physically assaulted, opposition leaders went into hiding; Endara found asylum in the papal *Nunciatura*.

With Noriega's brutal disregard for law and international opinion evident, President Bush and his advisers grew increasingly concerned about the physical safety of the thousands of U.S. citizens residing in Panama. In May he ordered nineteen hundred combat troops to Panama to protect the lives of U.S. citizens and property (Operation NIMROD DANCER). Nearly one thousand troops of the 7th Infantry Division (L) deployed to Panama in fifty-five sorties from Travis Air Force Base, California. One hundred and sixty-five members of the 2d Marine Expeditionary Force deployed from Camp Lejeune, North Carolina, by air within twenty-four hours. Finally, 762 troops of the 5th Infantry Division (Mechanized), from Fort Polk, Louisiana, moved by sea and arrived in Panama on 19 May.[13]

From the perspective of JTFPM and XVIIIth Airborne Corps planners, augmentation of JTFPM forces with NIMROD DANCER personnel would facilitate execution of BLUE SPOON. However, they did not view such augmentation as a definite commitment to execute BLUE SPOON. Policymakers and diplomats still hoped to persuade Noriega to resign and retire peacefully, but they underestimated his confidence and his obstinacy. Noriega's immediate reaction to NIMROD DANCER was defiance mixed with caution. On 18 May the PDF Department of National Investigation detained seventeen employees of a Panamanian company that provided security to the U.S. embassy. On 4 June, however, Noriega instructed the PDF to avoid confrontations with U.S. forces that might provide a pretext for invasion. Noriega specifically ordered the PDF to permit NIMROD DANCER convoys to travel unimpeded on legitimate roadways.[14]

A Get Tougher Policy: National Security Directive (NSD) 17

On 21 March 1989, former Congressman Dick Cheney succeeded Frank C. Carlucci as Secretary of Defense. Secretary Cheney met frequently with Secretary of State James Baker and the President's Assistant for National Security Affairs, retired Air Force Lieutenant General Brent Scowcroft. They sought new ways to pressure Noriega to retire. In addition to persuading other Latin American countries to censure Noriega, they considered signaling U.S. displeasure by reducing the number of U.S. military dependents in Panama while simultaneously augmenting the combat forces.[15]

During the spring and early summer, lower echelons of the National Security Council (NSC) met frequently to discuss such matters in detail. One such group, the Policy Coordinating Committee (PCC), comprised Bernard Aronson from the State Department, William Price from the National Security Council, Richard Brown from the Office of the Secretary of Defense (OSD), and Brigadier General David C. Meade, U.S. Army, from the Joint Staff. As Deputy Director for Politico-Military Affairs in the Directorate for Strategic Plans and Policy (J-5), General Meade informed the J-5, Lieutenant General George L. Butler, U.S. Air Force, of the options for removing Noriega: support of a Panamanian anti-Noriega coup, a U.S. covert operation to snatch the dictator, and major military operations in Panama. In General Meade's mind the process of deciding to oust Noriega began with the federal indictments: "Since February 1988, we had 'laid down a marker' that we wanted Noriega out. We [now] had options on how to do it....We could not execute those options [however] without a morally and legally acceptable justification as the catalyst."[16]

Interagency discussions culminated in NSD 17 being issued on 22 July 1989. In that document President Bush ordered military actions designed to assert U.S. treaty rights in Panama and to keep Noriega and his supporters off guard. Actions intended to accomplish the President's objective included Category I (Low Risk/Low Visibility) actions such as publicizing evacuation of U.S. dependents, expanding anti-Noriega campaigns in the media and in psychological operations, and placing members of the PDF under escort whenever they entered U.S. installations.[17]

In the remaining categories, U.S. troops in Panama would take more active roles. In Category II (Low Risk/High Visibility) military police would increase their patrols between U.S. installations, battalion-size forces would deploy to Panama for intensive training, Apache helicopters would conduct frequent training flights, and troops would practice amphibious and night combat operations. In Category III (Medium Risk/High Visibility) U.S. forces would increase their reconnaissance and armed convoys in the vicinity of important PDF installations. In Category IV (High Risk/High Visibility) U.S. troops would regain U.S. access to the causeway leading from Fort Amador toward the Canal Zone; and they would take control from the PDF of certain key facilities at Quarry Heights, Fort Amador, and Fort Espinar.[18]

New Leadership and New Plans

The impact of the President's decision to get tougher with Noriega became apparent in May 1989. President Bush turned from attempting to intimidate Noriega by a massive buildup of U.S. forces in Panama—the mass strategy followed during the Reagan years—to the surprise strategy. He also decided to replace one of the chief critics of the surprise strategy, General Woerner. Upon learning of the decision to replace Woerner, but not the reasons why, the Chief of Staff of the Army, General Carl E. Vuono, a close friend, flew to Panama to tell Woerner that the President had "decided to make a change" and that he should retire. At the end of July General Woerner met with Admiral Crowe and Secretary Cheney in Washington. The Secretary explained, "Fred, the President has decided to make a change....It has nothing to do with you or your performance. You did everything that we wanted you to do. It's political. It's just political."[19]

On 20 June, Admiral Crowe recommended General Maxwell R. Thurman, U.S. Army,[20] as General Woerner's replacement. A former Vice Chief of Staff of the Army, General Thurman was serving as Commanding General, U.S. Army Training and Doctrine Command, Fort Monroe, Virginia. On the verge of retiring, he enjoyed a reputation throughout the Army and the Joint Staff for uncommon vigor, aggressiveness, and determination to succeed. In the view of some Pentagon observers, Thurman's assignment signaled a shift in SOUTHCOM's focus from security assistance and diplomacy toward greater combat readiness.[21]

Admiral Crowe asked General Thurman to review the PRAYER BOOK operation orders, especially BLUE SPOON. On 4 August 1989, Thurman visited Fort Bragg, North Carolina, where he received three briefings: an overview followed by more detailed briefings on the JTFPM concept for conventional force operations and the Joint Special Operations Task Force (JSOTF) concept. As called for in the BLUE SPOON operation order of April 1988, the simultaneous conventional and special operations remained separate.[22]

Later in August, General Thurman and the SOUTHCOM J-3, Brigadier General William W. Hartzog, U.S. Army, conferred with Army Lieutenant General Carl W. Stiner, commander of the XVIIIth Airborne Corps. The three men noted that BLUE SPOON called for initial operations by the twelve thousand men already in Panama, staging in the United States of about ten thousand more troops, mostly from the 7th Infantry Division (L) over a five to six-day period, and their incremental deployment to Panama over the next fourteen days.[23]

Since BLUE SPOON had been published in April 1988, Noriega had become more defiant and his forces had become better equipped and better trained. A buildup over twenty-two days could mean prolonged conventional fighting, more casualties, and more opportunities for Noriega to take hostages or escape to the countryside to lead a guerrilla war. Structured primarily to conduct security assistance and military-to-military diplomacy, the SOUTHCOM operations staff was comparatively small and not suitable for the detailed planning and execution of the large, fast-moving operation that increasingly seemed likely.

The operations staff at the XVIIIth Airborne Corps had twice as many people as SOUTHCOM's; most of them were immersed in planning and training for rapid deployment and joint combat operations. As early as August 1989, General Thurman made up his mind that, upon taking command of SOUTHCOM in October, he would request that the XVIIIth Airborne Corps be designated at once (not after H-hour) as SOUTHCOM's primary planning and operational headquarters. Forewarned, Brigadier General Hartzog's staff began rewriting the operation order for BLUE SPOON "to sift out all the confusion that had been caused by eighteen months of evolution" and to include new guidance for the capture of Noriega. General Hartzog briefed the revised order, BANNER SAVIOR, to General Kelly on 15 September 1989.[24]

In August 1989, the President nominated Army General Colin L. Powell as Chairman of the Joint Chiefs of Staff beginning 1 October 1989. As Chairman, Powell would benefit from longstanding personal relationships with political leaders in both the Reagan and Bush administrations. Under Reagan, Powell, as National Security Adviser, had worked closely on Panamanian issues with Vice President Bush. As Commander in Chief, Forces Command, during the Bush presidency, Powell had worked on aspects of the burgeoning political crisis in Panama.

General Powell understood both the problems with BLUE SPOON and the deteriorating nature of the situation in Panama. During discussions with General Thurman and Lieutenant General Stiner in late September, General Powell agreed with three key points: (1) the timetable for BLUE SPOON must be compressed from three weeks to a few days, (2) U.S. forces should make a major effort to seize Noriega after H-hour, (3) more important, Joint Task Force South forces should make their primary military objective the disarming and dismantling of the Panama Defense Force. In General Powell's words, "if you're going to get tarred with a brush, you might as well take down the whole PDF...pull it up by the roots."[25]

The Failed Coup, 3 October 1989

On 1 October, Major Moisés Giroldi of the Panama Defense Force, who had helped suppress the coup attempt against Noriega in March 1988, proposed leading his own coup. He planned to seize PDF headquarters, *La Comandancia*, in Panama City the next day, rally anti-Noriega PDF units to him, and force Noriega to retire from office.

Giroldi and his partners sought to succeed Noriega's friends who monopolized the senior PDF positions.[26]

Using his wife as an emissary, Giroldi requested that SOUTHCOM place blocking forces on roads leading to Panama City from the PDF military bases at Rio Hato in western Panama and Fort Amador just southwest of the city. Along those routes Giroldi expected the 5th, 6th, and 7th PDF companies—loyal to Noriega—to advance to the *Comandancia* to rescue their leader. Giroldi also requested that his family be given sanctuary and that no U.S. aircraft fly near the *Comandancia* and give the impression that the United States was masterminding the coup. Giroldi warned that his men might shoot down such aircraft.

General Thurman did not trust Giroldi or his plan. Lacking time to check out Major Giroldi's claims, he feared that Giroldi might be setting the United States up to intervene blindly on behalf of a nonexistent coup in order to revive anti-American sentiment and Noriega's popularity. Even if the plan proved authentic, Thurman deprecated the idea of allowing Noriega to retire as a recipe for counterrevolution. In Thurman's words, the plan was "ill-conceived, ill-motivated, and ill-led."[27]

At 0238* Monday, 2 October, General Kelly informed the new Chairman of the Joint Chiefs of Staff that Giroldi would execute a coup against Noriega within the next five or six hours. Kelly also told General Powell that General Thurman strongly opposed employing U.S. combat forces to assist the coup plotters, at least until more was known about their plans and objectives. Within hours Powell and Secretary Cheney persuaded National Security Adviser Scowcroft, to avoid immediate commitment of U.S. military forces in support of the coup. That same day, however, Secretary Cheney authorized General Thurman to offer asylum to the families of the plotters and to prepare to assist the plotters with blocking forces if the President decided to grant Giroldi's request.

Upon learning that Noriega would not visit the *Comandancia* on 2 October, Giroldi postponed the coup until the next day. Meanwhile, General Thurman positioned some units near intersections west of the *Comandancia* for possible blocking operations. Thurman directed his troops not to fire unless in self-defense and not to block the intersections until he received specific orders from the President.[28]

On 3 October, the coup took place. With Noriega in hand, Giroldi repeatedly refused requests from General Cisneros to turn him over to

*Unless noted otherwise, times are Eastern Standard Time (EST).

SOUTHCOM for extradition to the United States. Meanwhile, in a move unanticipated by Major Giroldi, the 6th and 7th Rifle Companies flew over U.S. forces west of Panama City and entered the *Comandancia* from the east. Inside the *Comandancia* Noriega persuaded Giroldi to surrender. After being tortured and interrogated, Giroldi and his fellow officers were shot. Later, the Bush administration would come under heavy criticism for its apparent unwillingness or inability to assist Giroldi more forcefully.

General Thurman drew certain conclusions from the whole episode. The President, Secretary Cheney, and General Powell were quite right in offering only limited aid to the plotters. The United States should never base contingency planning for POST TIME or BLUE SPOON upon any coup by foreign nationals over whom it had no control. For a coup to succeed, massive U.S. military aid would be required, and the timing for D-Day and H-Hour would have to rest in U.S. hands, not those of the plotters. After Noriega's torture and slaying of Giroldi and his co-conspirators, very few PDF officers would be brave enough to risk another attempt. Even if some officers did, and succeeded with or without U.S. help, they probably would perpetuate the corruption of the Panama Defense Force as well as its monopoly of Panama's national security apparatus.[29]

Chapter 2

After the Coup Attempt:
Accelerated Joint Planning and Preparation
3 October–15 December 1989

General Thurman's Decisions, 3–20 October 1989

Following General Thurman's August discussions concerning the PRAYER BOOK operation orders, SOUTHCOM J-3 had begun revising BLUE SPOON. The J-3 staff planned to develop an entirely new operation order to be called BANNER SAVIOR, but there was not enough time. After assuming command on 30 September 1989 and witnessing the failure of Giroldi's coup, General Thurman anticipated that the President might order him to support another coup attempt by executing BLUE SPOON. Thurman instructed Brigadier General Hartzog to scrap plans for a new operation order and instead to expand the number of forces to deploy from the U.S. while compressing their "flow time" into Panama. General Powell agreed with that decision and stressed the need to be ready to execute the operation on very short notice.

To facilitate command and control, General Thurman provided for the early activation of Joint Task Force South (JTFSO) and on 10 October designated Lieutenant General Stiner as its commander. General Thurman told Army Chief of Staff General Vuono: "I want Stiner to be [my] warplanner, my warfighter."[1]

From 10 to 12 October 1989, General Stiner met with Hartzog, and the commander of the Joint Special Operations Task Force (JSOTF), Major General Gary E. Luck, U.S. Army, at SOUTHCOM headquarters. General Thurman directed the three generals to revise the command and control portion of BLUE SPOON with General Stiner in tactical command of all forces in Panama (JTFPM) and all conventional and special operations forces to be deployed there. He also directed the three generals to show how much of BLUE SPOON could be executed within 2 hours, 20 hours, and 48 hours of a coup attempt or some other "trigger event."[2]

In Washington to testify before two Senate committees concerning the Giroldi coup attempt, General Thurman met with the President and his advisers at the White House on 16 October. Those present included National Security Adviser Brent Scowcroft; Deputy National Security Adviser Robert Gates; John Sununu, the White House Chief of Staff; James Baker, the Secretary of State; Secretary Cheney; and General

Powell. General Thurman also met separately with General Powell and Lieutenant General Kelly to brief them on the progress being made revising BLUE SPOON. General Powell again stated that the task force must be fully prepared to "take down" the PDF which meant plenty of manpower and rehearsals. Powell later briefed Secretary Cheney who stressed the need to minimize casualties and the risk of U.S. civilians being taken hostage.[3]

General Thurman returned to Panama convinced that the national authorities wanted the United States to determine the trigger events for intervention rather than wait for Panamanian conspirators to select when and how the United States should help. To make the plan more flexible, Thurman approved a staggered interval concept that Stiner, Luck, and Hartzog briefed on 20 October. The concept offered scenarios for what could be accomplished within a period of twenty to forty-eight hours, using forces already in country, and within two to twenty hours using forces from the continental U.S. as well.[4]

The first scenario would, initially, use forces already in Panama. JTFPM forces would seize sites, interdict PDF units and airfields, and protect U.S. citizens and Panama Canal workers living in Panama Canal Commission (PCC) housing areas. Meanwhile, SOUTHCOM special operations forces would attempt to support the opposition, rescue hostages, and capture Noriega. Within twenty hours, Rangers from the U.S. would conduct additional offensive operations to seize the Tocumen Military Airfield outside Panama City. To provide adequate fire support for the initial assaults, especially within Panama City, SOUTHCOM would position Sheridan light tanks, Apache helicopters, and scout helicopters in Panama. Within forty-eight hours, Rangers and the 82d Airborne's Division Ready Brigade (DRB) would seize Tinajitas, Fort Cimarron, and Rio Hato and then shift to stability operations.[5]

A second scenario involved all BLUE SPOON forces, including those from the United States, at H-Hour. Within a period of two to twenty hours, conventional forces would protect and defend U.S. citizens and installations and interdict PDF airfields. Special operations forces would protect the opposition, seize the airfields, and neutralize the PDF command and control headquarters and facilities. Over the next twenty-eight hours the conventional forces would conduct stability operations.[6]

During the last ten days of October, the staffs at SOUTHCOM, at XVIIIth Airborne Corps, and at JSOTF headquarters drafted final plans. During the winter and spring of 1988 the SOUTHCOM J-3 had restricted access to BLUE SPOON planning documents, conversations, and conference calls. After the coup attempt of October 1989, and during the drafting of the final operational plans, FORSCOM operational security experts further restricted access; they insisted that each action officer receive only information relevant to his specific section of the overall plan.[7]

USCINCSO OPORD 1-90 (BLUE SPOON), 30 October 1989

General Hartzog and his staff completed revision of BLUE SPOON by 27 October. They increased the reinforcements from the continental U.S. by adding brigades from the 82d Airborne Division, the 7th Infantry Division (L), and units for the JSOTF including Rangers, Army Special Mission Units, and Navy Special Warfare Units. Altogether the revised BLUE SPOON would funnel twenty-seven thousand men into Panama within four to five days; the earlier version of the plan would have assembled a twenty-two thousand-man force over twenty-two days.[8]

New command arrangements blended flexibility and greater unity of command and control. If only in-place forces were available at H-Hour, they would work directly for USCINCSO who would act temporarily as the combat commander. When the JSOTF was committed, its commander would assume operational control over SOUTHCOM special operations forces. However, once General Stiner's headquarters and command were ready, General Thurman would activate Joint Task Force South (JTFSO). As COMJTFSO, General Stiner would assume command and control of all ground forces.

The revised BLUE SPOON (OPORD 1-90) summarized the support available to USCINCSO and COMJTFSO. In addition to directing the deployment and strategic airlift support, the Secretary of Defense would also direct support of the operation by the services, supporting unified and specified commands, and defense agencies. The services would provide logistic support and personnel augmentation for service components with each task force to include forces under the operational control of another service or in a joint command. The service components would be provided with a five-day basic load of consumable items and any equipment critical to air movement and ground combat. To regulate the loading and the flow of American forces to Panama, OPORD 1-90 provided for the establishment of a Joint Movement Control Center at Fort Bragg.

BLUE SPOON called for support of USCINCSO by four combatant commands. LANTCOM would provide naval and air coverage of the deploying forces and deter any Cuban or Nicaraguan attempts to interfere. In addition to the strategic airlift, TRANSCOM would provide sealift and terminal maintenance; FORSCOM would provide Army forces, civil affairs planners would be augmented by reservists and, later, a civil affairs brigade; SAC would take care of aerial refueling of deploying and covering aircraft and, on request from USCINCSO, would provide strategic reconnaissance. Also on request, the commander of the Air Force's Tactical Air Command (TAC) would deploy two Airborne Warning and Control System (AWACS) aircraft.

In addition to the State Department and the U.S. Information Agency (USIA), USCINCSO would receive support from four defense agencies. The Defense Intelligence Agency (DIA) would deploy a National Military Intelligence Support Team to link the Joint Staff with the intelligence staffs of USCINCSO, COMJTFSO, and COMJTFPM. The National Security Agency would deploy cryptographic elements, and the Defense Communications Agency and the Defense Mapping Agency would provide communications and mapping support.

BLUE SPOON 1-90 incorporated modified versions of the two scenarios that were briefed to USCINCSO on 20 October. In the "reactive execution" scenario, JTFPM forces already in Panama would react immediately to a trigger event such as the taking of U.S. hostages or attacks upon U.S. military installations or the Panama Canal. Conventional forces from the U.S. would execute their missions on arrival in Panama.

At H-Hour, JTFPM ground forces would secure Madden Dam, key defense sites, and PCC housing areas; prevent the Panama Defense Force from reinforcing Canal Zone operating areas and PDF headquarters at *La Comandancia*; and prevent Noriega's escape. Air support would strike or interdict important PDF facilities at Flamenco Island, Torrijos-Tocumen Airport, Rio Hato, Panama Viejo, Paitilla Airfield, and Tinajitas. At the same time, special operations forces—under a JSOTF—would conduct a number of operations: raids to capture Noriega; parachute assaults at Torrijos-Tocumen Airport and Rio Hato; operations against PDF forces at Flamenco Island, Balboa Harbor, Paitilla Airfield, Colón Harbor, and the Bridge of the Americas; and waterborne defense operations in the vicinity of Howard Air Force Base.

In the "deliberate execution" scenario, forces stationed in Panama and forces from the U.S. would conduct operations simultaneously. Planners noted that, "for political reasons, reactive execution is more likely, but deliberate is preferable." This scenario would allow at least sixty hours for TRANSCOM to execute the airlift; for JSOTF to conduct reconnaissance and surveillance of key targets such as Fort Cimarron, Tinajitas, Panama Viejo, and the Pacora River Bridge; and for FORSCOM to position more armor and aircraft in Panama.

Under deliberate execution, JSOTF would commence operations with five unconventional task forces. Task Force GREEN, the Army Special Mission Unit, would rescue a U.S. citizen imprisoned near the

Comandancia; while Task Force BLACK, SOUTHCOM's Special Forces, would protect opposition leaders. Task Force GREEN and Task Force BLUE, Army Special Mission and Navy Special Warfare units, would rescue any hostages; and Task Force WHITE, Navy Special Warfare Units, would conduct maritime operations against Panama City, Balboa Harbor, and Colón Harbor. Army Rangers made up Task Force RED and would conduct airborne assaults both at Rio Hato in the west and at Torrijos-Tocumen Airport in the east.

Deliberate execution would place three of four conventional task forces in action at H-Hour. Task Force BAYONET, the 193d Infantry Brigade, would seize the *Comandancia* and other PDF targets in Panama City and environs. Task Force ATLANTIC, the 7th Infantry Division (L) and the 82d Airborne Division, would seize sites in the Canal Zone from Panama City to Colón; and the Marines' Task Force SEMPER FI would concentrate on the land approaches to the Bridge of the Americas and Howard Air Force Base.

The operation was planned in four phases. At H+45 minutes Task Force PACIFIC—82d Airborne Division—would airdrop at Torrijos-Tocumen and relieve the Rangers. At H+90 minutes Task Force PACIFIC would capture or destroy PDF strongholds at Tinajitas, Fort Cimarron, and Panama Viejo. On the second day of operations, the 7th Infantry Division (L) and the 16th Military Police Brigade would complete deployment and commence stability operations. From D+3 to D+30 days, the 7th Infantry Division (L) would relieve all other combat units and together with the military police execute the civil-military plan, BLIND LOGIC.

During late October Generals Stiner, Luck, and Hartzog flew to Washington to brief OPORD 1-90 to General Kelly, General Powell, and the Joint Chiefs of Staff. Armed with charts, graphs, and after months of immersion in the planning, Hartzog provided what General Kelly later characterized as one of the best operations briefings he had ever heard. General Hartzog convinced General Powell that the plan was flexible and, barring a trigger event in the very near future, allowed ample time for rehearsals. General Powell liked the emphasis on using enough force to overwhelm the PDF in the shortest time possible. On 3 November, General Hartzog briefed the plan in "The Tank" to the Joint Chiefs of Staff. They agreed to it as written.[9]

After JCS approval of OPORD 1-90 on 3 November, Stiner, Luck, and Hartzog turned to refining the target lists and rehearsing plans for each of the task forces. Meanwhile, General Powell briefed Secretary Cheney and his deputy, Donald Atwood, on the plan. Secretary Cheney did not brief either the President or General Scowcroft on the details of BLUE SPOON; he did tell them that General Powell and his commanders were refining a plan for vigorous military intervention in

Panama. During the rehearsals over the next six weeks, the Secretary kept both men posted on special exercises or deployments that might prove embarrassing if revealed by the media.[10]

JTFSO OPLAN 90-2, 3 November 1989

Development of a detailed tactical plan took place at General Stiner's headquarters. On 3 November, while Stiner was in "The Tank" at the Pentagon, his chief planners at XVIIIth Airborne Corps headquarters completed JTFSO OPLAN 90-2 which included the particulars needed for a tactical operation. OPLAN 90-2 began with a statement of the commander's intent which focused on closing with and disarming the PDF.[11]

Leaving the details of special operations for the JSOTF to cover in its plan, XVIIIth Airborne Corps planners listed the targets for the Rangers and the four conventional task forces. Task Force RED, the Rangers, would assault Rio Hato and neutralize the PDF's 6th and 7th Rifle Companies (the units that had rescued Noriega during the last coup attempt). Task Force ATLANTIC, a brigade of 7th Infantry Division (L), would seize targets in the Canal Operating Zone from Gamboa to Colón and secure the Atlantic entrance to the Canal. Specific targets would include the electrical distribution center at Cerro Tigre, Madden Dam, and Renacer Prison in Gamboa. Task Force ATLANTIC would also protect U.S. installations in Colón, neutralize the 8th Rifle Company and a naval infantry unit, and seize both Coco Solo Naval Air Station and Fort Espinar.

Task Force PACIFIC, the Division Ready Brigade from the 82d Airborne Division and a Ranger battalion, would assault northeast of Panama City. The Rangers would begin the operation at H-Hour with an airdrop at Torrijos-Tocumen Airport. They would be followed in forty-five minutes by the paratroopers who would expand the airhead. Later, the task force would neutralize the PDF cavalry squadron at Panama Viejo, Battalion 2000 at Fort Cimarron, and the PDF's 1st Infantry Company at Tinajitas; it would also secure Cerro Azul and the airfield at Paitilla.

Two task forces would operate within Panama City and its western suburbs. Task Force BAYONET, the 193d Infantry Brigade, reinforced after 7 November by four Sheridan tanks, six Apache helicopters, three scout helicopters, and the 503d MP Battalion, would secure Fort Clayton, Quarry Heights, and Gorgas Military Hospital while pinning down the PDF's 5th Rifle Company at Fort Amador and the PDF forces in the *Comandancia*. Task Force BAYONET would also take control of the Carcel Modelo prison near the *Comandancia*. At the same time, Task Force SEMPER FI, one Marine rifle company, one Marine light armored vehicle company, and the Fleet Antiterrorist Support Team, would secure the Bridge of the Americas, the Thatcher Ferry Bridge Highway, and other western approaches to the Canal.

Army units numbered over twenty-two thousand troops. The Air Force contingent would number nearly thirty-four hundred, mostly units from the 830th Air Division. Air Force planes included two EF-111s for jamming, six EC-130s, eight AC-130 gunships, six F-117 Stealth fighter bombers, and other aircraft from the 1st Special Operations Wing. The next largest contingent would be about nine hundred Marines in Task Force SEMPER FI. The Navy would contribute over seven hundred men from Naval Special Warfare Group TWO, Naval Special Warfare Unit EIGHT, Special Boat Units 20 and 26, Countermine Division 127, and SEAL Teams TWO and FOUR.[12]

OPLAN 90-2 contained very precise rules of engagement (ROE). Commanders would ensure that troops used the minimum force necessary to accomplish military objectives. This guidance applied especially to the use of heavy weapons such as artillery, mortars, naval gunfire, tube-launched rockets, tank main guns, helicopter gunships, and AC-130 gunships. Use of these weapons in populated areas required approval by a ground commander in the grade of lieutenant colonel or commander. Bombardment or other attacks by heavy weapons against hospitals, medical unit facilities, schools, churches, museums, and historical monuments were prohibited except where such facilities were used by the enemy to conduct or support offensive operations. Attacks upon public works—dams, power plants, water purification facilities—were prohibited except when specifically authorized by General Stiner.

The public affairs annex to OPLAN 90-2 identified SOUTHCOM's Joint Information Office (JIO) as the chief coordinator and sole release authority for operational news. In support of the JIO, the JTFSO public affairs officer would coordinate the public affairs activities of JTFSO task forces and deny release of information concerning current or future operations, intelligence collection activities, friendly forces order of battle, and the effectiveness of enemy tactics and techniques.[13]

Lieutenant General Stiner had great confidence in the plan. He acknowledged that the 1988 version of BLUE SPOON laid much of the groundwork both for OPORD 1-90 and JTFSO OPLAN 90-2, but he believed that clear guidance from General Powell and General Thurman had expedited making the plan more flexible and efficient. Having briefed the plan to General Thurman and General Powell and the Joint Chiefs of Staff, General Stiner believed that the military chain of command understood the plan completely and would support its execution.[14]

Later General Powell made one significant change in the joint planning. After the Joint Chiefs of Staff approved OPORD 1-90 on 3 November, General Thurman had informed General Powell that he had established a Joint Deployment System (JDS) Plan Identification for special operations requirements. At SOCOM headquarters, the CINC, General James J. Lindsay, U.S. Army, worried that inclusion of such information in the JDS might make special operations visible to personnel who were not cleared for special operations planning. Lindsay was also concerned that his staff lacked the experience necessary for making the transition from planning small, closely-held operations to the kind of planning necessary for the JDS. On the other hand, General Stiner questioned whether the JDS could accommodate the detailed data, such as hours and minutes instead of days, necessary to execute the operation. Confronted with objections from two major commanders, General Powell decided to exclude OPORD 1-90 from the Joint Deployment System. Because TRANSCOM depended heavily upon the JDS for its planning, General Powell's decision effectively removed TRANSCOM from supporting the operation and made its Air Force component, Military Airlift Command (MAC), responsible for strategic airlift.[15]

Rehearsals and a Bomb Threat, 7 October–15 December 1989

Four days after failure of the Giroldi coup, General Thurman initiated training and meetings to prepare his command for action. On 7 October, he ordered Major General Cisneros to test all JTFPM units, from squad to battalion level, with live fire exercises. When he learned that these units had not conducted live fire exercises in some time, General Thurman insisted that all units remain in the field until they had qualified with every weapon in their inventory. Throughout the remainder of October and into November, planning staffs met at Quarry Heights and at Fort Bragg to refine coordination procedures, develop joint execution checklists, and joint communications instructions. They also planned post-D-Day operations.[16]

The most significant of those joint planning conferences took the form of a seminar at Fort Clayton, Panama, on 18 November. General Thurman reviewed with General Stiner, General Cisneros, General Luck, and SOUTHCOM Air Force and Navy component commanders, the actions each would take during a reactive execution, after a trigger event, and during a deliberate execution after substantial advance notice.[17]

During the days preceding the conference at Fort Clayton, General Thurman had learned of an alleged plot by the Medellín drug cartel to attack U.S. defense facilities in Panama during the week of Thanksgiving,19–24 November, in reprisal for the U.S. counternarcotics program. The attack would be carried out with the assistance of two of Noriega's top lieutenants, Major Mario Del Cid in Colón and Major Victor Herrerra in Bocas Del Toro.[18]

While the bomb threat would prove to be a hoax, General Thurman acted to protect his command. The idea of a massacre of U.S. troops by car bomb, as had happened to the U.S. Marines in Beirut in 1983, horrified and angered Thurman. He was determined that such an attack would not succeed "on his watch." He speculated that, if he failed, the loss of American lives would cause President Bush to order execution of BLUE SPOON. After conclusion of the seminar on 18 November, Thurman took General Stiner aside and formally "activated Joint Task Force South for planning." General Thurman also initiated stringent security checks at all U.S. installations and stepped up the tempo of exercises and rehearsals during the next three weeks. In Panama, General Cisneros increased the number of exercises and troop movements in BLUE SPOON ("Sand Flea exercises") operational areas. At Fort Benning, Georgia, and in Panama, General Stiner rehearsed the Ranger battalions.[19]

Powell briefed Cheney on those developments. The Secretary later remarked. "We adopted a more aggressive posture. We sent U.S. forces up and down the causeways, conducted helicopter operations, and scheduled exercises." In the Secretary's opinion the heightened pace of exercises pushed General Stiner's forces to a high state of readiness; increased the tension and incidents between U.S. and PDF troops; and, by their frequency, caused Noriega to believe that the U.S. was trying to intimidate him. Consequently, Noriega did not expect an attack.[20]

Chapter 3

Trigger Events, The Decision to Intervene, and Final Preparations for H-Hour
15–16 December 1989

Trigger Events, 15-16 December 1989

Increased tension between U.S. and PDF forces culminated in provocative declarations by the Panamanian leadership. On Friday, 15 December, the National Assembly passed a resolution stating that "owing to U.S. aggression," a state of war existed with the United States. That same day Noriega named himself the Maximum Leader and publicly speculated that someday the "bodies of our enemies" would float down the Panama Canal and the people of Panama would win complete control over the waterway.[1]

Violent acts followed the next day. During the evening, four U.S. officers, apparently on a Saturday night outing, took a wrong turn and approached a PDF checkpoint at the *Comandancia*. At about 2110, guards from the Panama Defense Force stopped the car and tried to force the officers outside. When the Americans refused to leave their vehicle, a PDF soldier loaded a magazine into his AK-47; the car pulled away. As the guard fired, the car sped off, only to approach another PDF guardpost. The soldiers there also began firing. Their bullets wounded three of the officers in the car; one of them, Marine First Lieutenant Robert Paz, died of his wounds in the Gorgas Military Hospital.

While the U.S. officers were trying to escape, a U.S. couple who witnessed the incident, a junior U.S. naval officer and his wife, were brought to a police station for questioning. Interrogators kicked the officer in the groin, hit him in the mouth, and pointed a gun at his head. Other PDF members forced his wife to stand against a wall while they groped her; she collapsed.[2]

At 2125, SOUTHCOM notified General Kelly of the shooting. Kelly notified General Powell and alerted the commanders of the XVIIIth Airborne Corps, MAC, and the JSOTF. Powell informed Rear Admiral William A. Owens, Senior Military Assistant to Secretary Cheney; on learning of the incident, Secretary Cheney called Brent Scowcroft. General Thurman and his executive assistant, Colonel James F. Hennessee, were in Washington; they learned of the shooting incident at 2230. When General Powell asked General Thurman what he was going to do, Thurman said he would fly to Panama and determine the facts before making a recommendation. Thurman and his executive officer boarded a jet at 0100 on 17 December.[3]

Key Military Meetings, Sunday Morning, 17 December 1989

General Thurman and Colonel Hennessee arrived at Howard Air Force Base in Panama at 0600 and went directly to the SOUTHCOM operations center, "the Tunnel," where General Hartzog briefed them. General Thurman then called Powell and outlined three options: do nothing, try to seize Noriega in a snatch operation, or execute Operation BLUE SPOON. General Thurman told the Chairman that after two months of intensive planning and rehearsals, SOUTHCOM, JTFSO, and the JSOTF were ready to implement the third option.[4]

During the morning of 17 December, General Powell consulted with two other commanders and the Secretary of Defense. From 0900 to 0945 he spoke with the commanders of the JSOTF and MAC and asked how soon they could be ready to execute the airlift and special operations in Panama. They needed forty-eight hours. General Powell then met with Secretary Cheney, Under Secretary of Defense for Policy Paul Wolfowitz, and representatives from the National Security Council. According to General Powell, most of the policy advisers were uneasy about whether the shooting at the *Comandancia* constituted "enough of a smoking gun" to go to war. They feared that the "accidental blundering" of the four officers into the vicinity of the *Comandancia* might appear to be a reconnaissance or even a provocation.

Convinced that the incident had been accidental, Secretary Cheney had fewer qualms about taking strong action against Noriega and the PDF, especially after General Powell reminded him that BLUE SPOON had been refined and General Thurman's forces could not be better prepared to execute it. The Secretary decided to brief the President and his key advisers that afternoon and called National Security Adviser Scowcroft to arrange the presentation.[5]

Before accompanying Secretary Cheney to the meeting with the President, General Powell conferred with the Joint Chiefs of Staff. To avoid alerting the press, he invited his colleagues to join him at Fort Myer. The meeting began in General Powell's quarters at 1130. In addition to the Service Chiefs, the Vice Chairman, Air Force General Robert T. Herres, General Kelly, and Rear Admiral Edward D. Sheafer, also attended. On hearing of the shooting and death of Marine Lieutenant Paz, the Joint Chiefs of Staff, especially the Commandant of the Marine Corps, were convinced that the killing of a U.S. serviceman should not go unanswered. After General Kelly and Admiral Sheafer reviewed BLUE SPOON and the intelligence situation, the Joint Chiefs of Staff agreed that, if the President wanted to intervene, BLUE SPOON provided a good plan.[6]

Decision at the White House, Sunday Afternoon, 17 December 1989

Before leaving for the White House, Powell and Kelly carefully reviewed the pattern of escalating Panamanian harassment and violence during the last two months. The review showed that the shootings and beatings at the *Comandancia* on 16 December were not isolated incidents. This point would be central in any discussion of using military force in Panama. The meeting with the President, General Scowcroft, Mr. Gates, Secretary Baker, Secretary Cheney, and the White House Press Secretary, Marlin Fitzwater, began at 1430. Secretary Cheney discussed the events of Friday and Saturday night. General Kelly then reviewed in broad outline the concept of operations and the forces for BLUE SPOON.[7]

In considering a military operation of the scope of BLUE SPOON, President Bush and his counselors discussed its broad objectives. The planners for BLUE SPOON, both on the Joint Staff and at SOUTHCOM, had wrestled with the question of its political objectives. The answers reemerged during the course of the White House discussion that Sunday afternoon: to safeguard the lives of nearly 30,000 U.S. citizens residing in Panama; to protect the integrity of the Panama Canal and 142 U.S. defense sites; to help the Panamanian opposition establish genuine democracy; to neutralize the PDF; and, to bring Noriega to justice.

Initially President Bush's interest in a military operation was guarded. He wanted assurance that it would not backfire as had the attempted rescue of U.S. hostages in Iran during the Carter administration. He also wanted to preclude the interservice problems that arose in 1983 during the intervention in Grenada. The President asked: "Would the plan work? Did it have to be that big? How many casualties would there be? How much damage would be done? What would be the diplomatic consequences throughout Latin America?"

General Powell explained that even if U.S. intelligence could locate Noriega, an operation to snatch him would not solve the problems with Panama. The entire PDF leadership was corrupt, and there were Noriega clones who could replace him. The entire PDF must be dismantled. That could be accomplished, General Powell said, most effectively with a massive military operation to neutralize the PDF as the first step toward its reconstruction. Even if Noriega escaped, he would have lost his power base and eventually would be captured. Moreover, General Powell concluded a massive intervention would minimize the time available for the PDF to seize U.S. citizens. Needing no further persuasion, President Bush ordered execution of BLUE SPOON with the words: "Okay, let's do it. The hell with it!"

After the President approved execution of BLUE SPOON, General Powell and General Kelly returned to the Pentagon to transform the operation from a paper concept into the movement of thousands of troops and tons of materiel over hundreds of miles to the isthmus of Panama. At 1630 General Kelly briefed his top planners and advisers within J-3 on the President's decision; he directed them to set up a Crisis Action Team in the Crisis Management Room of the National Military Command Center (NMCC) no later than Tuesday, 19 December.[8]

General Kelly also told his staff that General Stiner wanted H-Hour at 0100 on the morning of 20 December. That timing permitted Stiner to begin his operations at night. The airborne and special operations troops were better trained and equipped for night operations than any other comparable force in the world. Kelly said: "We own the night. We're the best night fighters on earth." Major General James D. Kellim, U.S. Air Force, the Director of Operations for MAC, agreed to the timing because it provided him with the nearly sixty hours to launch the airlift. From 1700 to about 1730 General Powell and General Kelly telephoned key commanders and their directors of operations to tell them of the President's decision and that a written execute order would follow. After the calls General Kelly asked General Powell to authorize Major General Wayne A. Downing, U.S. Army, JSOTF Commander, to begin preparations for pre-H-Hour insertion of special operations forces. By 1930 that evening General Powell notified Kelly that Secretary Cheney had approved the request and JSOTF movement could begin within the half hour.[9]

Monday, 18 December 1989: Movement Preparation, the F-117A Decision, and the Execute Order

After JSOTF movements had begun, the XVIIIth Airborne Corps began movement preparation. At midnight on 17 December the chief of staff of XVIIIth Airborne Corps led the JTFSO advance party to Panama. Upon arrival the party moved into the U.S. Army South Emergency Operations Center (EOC), Fort Clayton, to establish JTFSO (Forward). At 1500 on 18 December, General Stiner and his principal staff deployed to the forward headquarters. The establishment of the tactical commander in the operational area and the arrival of supporting staff and units on 19 December would greatly facilitate General Stiner's control of the assault forces when they landed.

Meanwhile, MAC commenced movement preparations on 18 December. Aircraft at Charleston Air Force Base, South Carolina, Pope Air Force Base, North Carolina, Hunter Army Airfield and Lawson Army Airfield, Georgia, were configured for airlifting equipment and troops. Airmen rigged, loaded, and moved heavy equipment away from home stations to make room on the ramp for aircraft carrying personnel. Crews executed schedules for loading and staggered takeoffs on 19 December, D-Day minus 1.[10]

The Secretary of Defense followed the tactical execution of BLUE SPOON closely. He wanted to avoid repeating the mistakes that had plagued earlier contingency operations in Grenada and Lebanon. Cheney listened carefully as Powell and Kelly explained the execute order that they were preparing for transmission later that day. Their explanation satisfied the Secretary that the chain of operational command was as "short and clean as possible"; that interservice logrolling had been avoided—with only those forces best suited for the operation being tasked; and that the commanders and their troops thoroughly understood the rules of engagement.[11]

Secretary Cheney questioned and changed only the provision in OPORD 1-90 to employ six F-117A stealth aircraft against Rio Hato and the two possible Noriega hideouts, La Escondida and Boquete. He said, "Come on, guys, how severe is the Panama air defense threat?" Once the press broke the story of the use of the F-117A, he knew that Congress would criticize the White House and the Pentagon for an opportunistic use of the plane to justify its expense.[12]

The Chairman and General Kelly laid out the reasons why General Stiner had asked for the aircraft: to stun rather than kill the PDF troops at Rio Hato and to provide airborne troops assaulting La Escondida and Boquete with the best available nighttime close air support. The case for Rio Hato was especially persuasive. The PDF's elite 6th and 7th Rifle Companies there had saved Noriega during the October coup attempt; yet many of the rank and file were known to be friendly to the United States. To kill them with ordinary bombing or gunfire might stiffen resistance throughout Panama. The rules of engagement clearly sought to avoid that situation. General Stiner believed that by dropping bombs no closer than 150 yards from the barracks, the explosion and the subsequent call for surrender by Rangers surrounding the barracks would induce the Panamanians to surrender after token resistance.[13]

Stiner's exacting requirements meant that other aircraft would not do. Air Force AC-130 gunships would require too much flight time from the U.S. and could not be relied upon to fight effectively below a cloud cover of ten thousand feet. Apache gunships could do the job, but those available would be needed to take the *Comandancia*. General

Stiner turned to his supporting Air Force commander, Lieutenant General Peter T. Kempf, 12th Air Force. Kempf recommended the F-117A. Designed to fly at night, it could drop 2,000-pound laser-guided bombs with great precision.

After presenting Stiner's case, General Powell nonetheless asked General Thurman to review the need for strikes at Rio Hato, La Escondida, and Boquete. Thurman made a strong argument for bombing near the PDF barracks at Rio Hato. Both General Powell and Secretary Cheney agreed on the need for a strike there and on 19 October persuaded the President. Neither Powell nor Cheney accepted the argument for using the F-117A against Noriega's hideouts at La Escondida and Boquete. The original plan—to use special operations forces to capture Noriega at either place, but if he was not there to bypass both—made more sense.

Around 1050, General Kelly briefed the Chairman on the execute order; then the Chairman reviewed it with the Joint Chiefs of Staff. All were satisfied, and the message was sent at 1825. On receiving the execute order, FORSCOM sent a message at 2000 to the commander of the XVIIIth Airborne Corps, directing him to execute the order with the 82d Airborne and 7th Infantry Division (L) under his operational control and, if necessary, the 24th Infantry Division (Mechanized).[14]

The provisions of the order, except for those concerning the F-117As, were virtually identical to the briefing General Hartzog had presented in "The Tank" on 3 November. The order did, however, announce a new name for the operation. The previous evening General Lindsay, USCINCSOC, and General Kelly had discussed the name and Lindsay asked whether Kelly wanted to tell his grandchildren that he had participated in Operation BLUE SPOON. While BLUE SPOON had been quite satisfactory during the planning stage, General Kelly agreed that the time had come to provide a name that would underscore the purpose of the operation and inspire the forces and the people back home. General Kelly discussed changing the name of the operation to JUST ACTION. Instead, he changed the name to JUST CAUSE; General Powell agreed.[15]

Tuesday, 19 December 1989: Launching the Airlift

On Tuesday, 19 December, General Powell met with President Bush before U.S. troops began their airlift into Panama. Meeting at 1400, the Chairman reviewed the execute order with the President and gave him the opportunity to make some last minute decisions. If the President had any qualms about the operation, this was the time to call it off. Bush held firm. He assured Powell that, even if Endara, Arias

Calderón, and Ford balked at setting up a new Panamanian government, he would not postpone or cancel the operation. President Bush approved the employment of two F-117As at Rio Hato, saying "They're American troops. Give them what they need." Finally, the President announced his intention to explain to Congress and the press the purpose and nature of JUST CAUSE early the next morning. After General Powell briefed the Joint Chiefs of Staff at 1430, he telephoned General Thurman at Quarry Heights telling him, "It's a go...Good luck!"[16]

The airlift began on 19 December with Rangers from Fort Lewis, Washington, who departed Lawson Army Airfield in thirteen C-130s at 1316. Rangers from Fort Stewart, Georgia, departed from Hunter Army Airfield in twelve C-130s at 1432. Later, at 1554, the remainder of thirty C-141 heavy drop cargo aircraft that had not already left flew out of Charleston Air Force Base.[17]

Carrying two battalions of the 82d Airborne Division from Fort Bragg, twenty C-141s were supposed to depart Pope Air Force Base for Panama shortly after the Rangers' airlift. Freezing rain and repeated icing of the wings prevented them from taking off on time. Using all available deicers, ground crews readied ten C-141s for takeoff at 2045. The other ten followed nearly four and one-half hours later. The commander of the 82d Airborne Division asked permission to delay arrival time of the first serial until both battalions could drop together. Sticking as closely as possible to the original timetable, General Stiner ordered the commander to drop his men in two separate serials as soon as each reached the target area.[18]

Over 200 aircraft participated in the deployment to Panama. MAC aircraft directly involved in carrying troops and equipment numbered 80 C-141s, 22 to 25 C-130s, and 11 C-5s. The Strategic Air Command contributed KC-10s and KC-135s to refuel MAC aircraft as well as supporting reconnaissance missions. During the airflow to Panama and back to the United States, sixteen F-15s and four F-16s, from the U.S. Atlantic Command Air Force component, AFLANT, flew combat air patrols from Key West over the Caribbean between the Yucatan Peninsula and Cuba. Their mission was to deter or interdict attempts by Cuba or Nicaragua to interfere with or attack the airlift. The F-15s protected ingress; the F-16s protected egress. Naval aircraft from the Atlantic Fleet provided search and rescue coverage. Finally, Air Force E-3 AWACS provided aerial surveillance, threat warning, fighter control, air situation updates, control of air refueling operations, and back up for search and rescue operations.[19]

The massive movement of U.S. aircraft to Panama in the afternoon and evening of 19 December compromised strategic surprise. Upon receipt of the execute order, General Stiner's headquarters announced an emergency deployment readiness exercise in an unsuccessful attempt to explain the airlift as just another exercise. At 2200 on the evening of 19 October, Dan Rather of CBS News commented: "U.S. military transport planes have left Fort Bragg. The Pentagon declines to say whether or not they're bound for Panama. It will say only that the Fort Bragg-based 18th Airborne Corps has been conducting what the Army calls an emergency readiness measure."

Intelligence sources in SOUTHCOM began picking up evidence that personnel at the *Comandancia* were aware of the movement of C-130s and C-141s into Howard Air Force Base as early as 1700. The PDF leaders apparently took precautionary steps to respond to a U.S. military operation against them, but were not certain what type of action it would be and when it would begin. At about 1727 Del Cid, a key Noriega subordinate in Panama City, speculated that the U.S. forces were planning a surgical strike to seize Noriega. By 1849 PDF headquarters had alerted the elite PDF Battalion 2000 stationed near the Torrijos-Tucumen Airport and some other units as well. It had also placed key bases and sectors of Panama under blackout.[20]

By 2000 intelligence sources picked up evidence that the PDF had its first inkling of H-Hour. A PDF soldier reported that he had overheard two U.S. troops conversing in Spanish about H-Hour being at 0100. At 2158 the *Comandancia* ordered all units to report by telephone every thirty minutes. Two hours later, the *Comandancia* sent out a message, probably to some of the troop commanders: "They're coming. The ballgame is at 1 AM. Report to your units...draw your weapons and prepare to fight." Another message went out to the Rio Hato military complex at 2330: "Draw your weapons and get out on the airfield; start shooting when they come over; block the runways."

The press claimed two other breaches of operational security. Both claims proved baseless. In one, a U.S. official allegedly called a friend and warned: "Tonight is the night. One o'clock is the time. Get your kids off the street; make certain they're home." The second breach allegedly involved a burst radio transmission from Cuba to Panama warning of the approaching invasion. General Powell and General Kelly later noted that the first report had been investigated but never proven. General Kelly verified that a burst transmission went out from Panama to Cuba. If it was an effort to alert Cuba, Cuban forces and radar failed to react. The airlift flew undetected below Cuban radar coverage.[21]

General Stiner believed that security breaches had denied his forces tactical surprise. Some PDF troops, possibly sentries, fired upon the Rangers as they dropped over Rio Hato. The lack of widespread effective resistance he attributed to Noriega and his advisers' misreading U.S. intentions. General Stiner believed that either Noriega and his advisers did not trust their own information, or they were too incompetent to take the measures necessary to mount a proper defense throughout Panama.[22]

General Powell, General Kelly, and Assistant Secretary of Defense for Public Affairs Lewis A. "Pete" Williams, characterized the PDF as not reacting to hard intelligence about H-Hour as much as taking precautionary measures in the wake of reports of the airlift. If the PDF had truly been alerted, according to General Kelly, they would have distributed .50 caliber machine guns and other antiaircraft weapons throughout Panama that same evening. They might also have begun taking U.S. citizens hostage at the Holiday Inn and the Mariott. They might have issued a general alert that evening instead of the next day, hours after H-Hour. If Noriega had expected an invasion at 0100, he might have spent his evening at a command and control facility or a hideout rather than in the home of a prostitute.[23]

On the evening of the airlift, the Commander of the Joint Special Operations Task Force (COMJSOTF), Major General Downing, elaborated on the instructions to his subordinate task forces to locate and apprehend Noriega either in the air or on the ground. If intelligence, radar, or AWACS detected Noriega attempting to escape by air, AC-130 gunships or F-16 fighters would intercept his aircraft and order it to land. If the pilot refused to obey the order, the U.S. military aircraft, upon authorization from Secretary Cheney, would shoot down the suspect aircraft. If U.S. intelligence located Noriega at one of his hideouts such as Altos de Golfo, or La Escondida, Task Force GREEN, the Army's Special Mission Unit, would employ "snatch teams" supported by UH-60 helicopters or AC-130 gunships to assault the hideout and capture Noriega.[24]

While special operations forces searched for Noriega, U.S. diplomatic and military officials in Panama City prepared to install a new civilian government. Earlier on 19 December, the U.S. Deputy Chief of Mission in Panama, John Bushnell, had invited to dinner at his quarters on Howard Air Force Base, President Guillermo Endara, First Vice President Ricardo Arias Calderón, and Second Vice President Guillermo "Billy" Ford all of whom had been legally elected in May 1989. Shortly after arriving at Howard, the three Panamanians boarded helicopters at 2130 for a flight to SOUTHCOM headquarters at Quarry Heights. General Thurman and Mr. Bushnell briefed the politicians on JUST CAUSE and offered them the opportunity to assume their elected offices and lead the effort to set up a new government. Endara, Arias Calderón, and Ford accepted and were sworn in by a Panamanian judge just before midnight.[25]

Chapter 4

D-Day, Wednesday, 20 December 1989

Opposing Forces

The Panamanian Defense Force numbered nearly 12,800 troops, national guard, police, and officials; but only about 4,000 could be classified as combat troops. The ground forces of the Panama Defense Force were organized into 2 infantry battalions, 5 light infantry companies, 1 cavalry troop, and 2 public order companies; their equipment included 28 armored cars. The PDF air force comprised five hundred troops with an assortment of reconnaissance, transport, and training planes as well as unarmed helicopters. The PDF navy numbered four hundred sailors equipped with a handful of patrol craft, cutters, and launches. In addition, Noriega's forces included up to eighteen paramilitary Dignity Battalions.[1]

Based upon the performance of the PDF units during the abortive Giroldi coup, General Thurman expected particular resistance from the following units: Battalion 2000, about 550 troops at Fort Cimarron, 15 miles east of Panama City; 2d Infantry Company, about 200 troops at Torrijos-Tocumen Airport; 1st Infantry Company, about 200 troops at Tinajitas just north of Panama City; 5th Rifle Company, about 300 troops at Fort Amador near the Bridge of the Americas southwest of Panama City; 12th Cavalry Squadron, about 150 troopers at Panama Viejo between Panama City and Fort Cimarron; 8th Rifle Company, about 175 men at Fort Espinar in the Colón area; 6th and 7th Rifle Companies, about 400 troops at Rio Hato; and elements of the 6th, 7th, and 8th Companies, about 150 troops at the *Comandancia*.[2]

Before H-Hour, American forces in Panama numbered nearly thirteen thousand troops, including the 193d Infantry Brigade, a battalion from the 7th Infantry Division (L), a mechanized battalion from the 5th Infantry Division (M), two companies of Marines, and an assortment of military police, Air Force, and Navy personnel. On and shortly after H-Hour, the airlift brought in a strike force of seven thousand troops: a composite brigade of the 82d Airborne Division, the 75th Infantry Regiment (Ranger), and the equivalent of five or six battalions of other special operations forces that included Army Special Forces, Navy Sea-Air-Land forces (SEALs), Navy special boat units, Air Force special operations personnel and psychological operations specialists.[3]

Later on D-Day, and during the next few days, an additional seven thousand troops—mostly from the 7th Infantry Division (L) and the 16th Military Police Brigade and various civil affairs and psychological operations units—arrived to relieve the assault forces, engage in stability operations, and help establish the new government. The last increment brought to twenty-seven thousand the total of U.S. forces in Panama for JUST CAUSE; nearly twenty-two thousand actually engaged in combat operations as members of the conventional task forces, ATLANTIC, PACIFIC, BAYONET, SEMPER FI, or of the unconventional warfare task forces, GREEN, BLACK, BLUE, WHITE, and RED.[4]

Actions by the Special Operations Forces

Unusual PDF activity after midnight on 20 December prompted General Stiner to advance H-Hour. The PDF headquarters warned the commander at Rio Hato to block the runways; shooting occurred at the *Comandancia*; a U.S. female dependent was shot and wounded at Albrook Air Force Station; more firing was heard at Fort Amador and at the Bridge of the Americas; the PDF headquarters received a report of an attack on a vehicle; and the Dignity Battalions were alerted to report to their respective military zone commanders. To prevent total loss of tactical surprise, General Stiner ordered the special operations forces to launch their operations fifteen minutes ahead of schedule, at 0045.[5]

Special operations forces struck simultaneously at several targets. One unit assaulted the Carcel Modelo prison at the *Comandancia*. During an attack on the Punta Paitilla Airport, Navy SEALs lost four men as they encountered unexpectedly stiff resistance. Other special operations forces successfully secured the Pecora River Bridge to prevent reinforcements from reaching the garrison at Torrijos-Tocumen Airport. Special Forces teams unsuccessfully sought Noriega at a Pacific coast villa and at the home of a mistress.[6]

Meanwhile, the pilots of the two F-117As flew to Rio Hato to drop one 2,000-pound bomb each within 150 yards of the PDF's 6th and 7th Rifle Company barracks to stun and confuse the occupants just before Rangers of Task Force RED parachuted into the area. Upon reaching the target area, the pilots encountered high winds coming from an unanticipated direction. The lead pilot swung to the left, and dropped his payload only sixty yards away from the barracks that was supposed to be the near target of the pilot in the second aircraft. Keying on the first pilot, the second pilot dropped his bomb further to the left, up to three hundred yards away from the target that had been originally assigned to the lead pilot. Despite the error, the bombs exploded precisely where aimed and momentarily stunned the PDF troops occupying the barracks.[7]

At 0100, nearly thirteen hundred Rangers of Task Force RED jumped over targets from Rio Hato in the west to Fort Cimarron in the east. Within the next forty-five minutes an additional twenty-seven hundred troopers from the 82d Airborne Division joined the Rangers in the largest U.S. airborne operation since World War II. The Rangers and paratroopers had the primary mission of isolating Panama City while assault forces within Panama City encircled and neutralized PDF headquarters at the *Comandancia*. Both Rangers and paratroopers dropped from five hundred feet or below, three hundred feet lower than practice drops in the U.S. Exiting at a lower jump altitude and, often in the face of ground fire, some of the men forgot to release their heavy rucksacks. They landed hard and a number of soldiers injured their ankles.[8]

Within minutes of jumping at Rio Hato and Torrijos-Tocumen Airport, the Rangers engaged in some of the heaviest fighting on D-Day. At Rio Hato, the troops of the PDF's 6th and 7th Rifle Companies managed to overcome the shock of the F-117A strikes and fight for over five hours before 250 surrendered. Another group of 150 to 240 Panamanian soldiers fled into the countryside. At Torrijos-Tocumen Airport a Ranger battalion assaulted at 0124 and engaged the PDF's 1st Infantry Company. At 0145 initial elements of the ready brigade of the 82d Airborne Division parachuted into the area. Delayed by icing in North Carolina, ten aircraft arrived with the remainder of the brigade after 0500. The Ranger and airborne troops at Torrijos-Tocumen Airport then combined as Task Force PACIFIC.

By 0730, troops from Task Force PACIFIC had cleared the airport of the 1st Infantry Company, about fifty of whom surrendered. While the Rangers and paratroopers set up a security perimeter, General Noriega and his driver drove up to one of their roadblocks. General Noriega had just come from a tryst with a prostitute. The sight of paratroopers dropping nearby compelled him to change his plans for the evening. Spotting the paratroopers at the roadblock, Noriega ordered his driver to turn around and go the other way.[9]

The Conventional Task Forces

At 0100, Task Force ATLANTIC—a battalion from the 7th Infantry Division (L) and one from the 82d Airborne Division—attacked into the Colón-Gamboa sector extending southeast from the Atlantic entrance of the Panama Canal midway to Panama City. After fighting PDF's 8th Rifle Company at Fort Espinar and the naval infantry company at Coco

Solo Naval Air Station, the battalion from the 7th Infantry Division (L) secured the electrical distribution center at Cerro Tigre, Fort Davis, France Hospital, Madden Dam, and the Gatun Locks. The battalion from the 82d Airborne Division captured the Renacer Prison at Gamboa where it freed 64 prisoners including 7 PDF officers and 2 U.S. citizens. Task Force ALANTIC reported all missions accomplished by 1029; they had killed 22 enemy soldiers, wounded 22, and captured 158, but believed that up to 250 PDF troops had escaped.[10]

Task Force SEMPER FI, a Marine rifle company and a Marine light armored vehicle company, commenced operations at H-Hour in the western suburbs of Panama City. They captured PDF stations at Vera Cruz and Arraijan and secured the area surrounding Howard Air Force Base. Their primary mission, however, was to occupy the approaches to the Bridge of the Americas, a vital choke point along the main roads for PDF forces fleeing Rio Hato with possible intent of reinforcing the *Comandancia*. Having killed 2 PDF troops, wounded 2, and captured 15, Task Force SEMPER FI regrouped at 0700 to attack the headquarters of the 10th Military Zone in La Chorrera.[11]

Task Force BAYONET faced perhaps the greatest challenge on D-Day. Supported by four Sheridan armored reconnaissance and assault vehicles and helicopter gunships, three battalions (5–87th Infantry, 1–508th Infantry [Airborne], and 4–6th Infantry [Mechanized]) at 0100 moved through the sprawling urban area of Panama City to capture Fort Amador, seize the *Comandancia*, and protect the U.S. embassy. The U.S. embassy began receiving rocket propelled grenades and mortar fire at 0134; the attacks ceased when U.S. forces reached the compound around 0415. At Fort Amador, PDF's 5th Rifle Company held out against Task Force BAYONET until 1029.[12]

At the *Comandancia*, elements of PDF's 6th, 7th, and 8th Rifle Companies, reinforced by the two public order companies, vigorously defended PDF headquarters for nearly three hours. Defenders shot down two U.S. special operations helicopters and forced one observation helicopter to ditch in the Panama Canal. With direct fire support from the Sheridans and helicopters, the troops of Task Force BAYONET destroyed much of the *Comandancia* building and eventually won the day. The Hellfire missiles of the Apache helicopters were so accurate that, according to General Stiner, "You could fire that Hellfire missile through a window four miles away at night." During the fighting, Task Force BAYONET killed 24, wounded 9, and captured 463 PDF troops.[13]

Casualties and damage would have been greater in Panama City if General Stiner had not strictly enforced the JUST CAUSE rules of engagement that sharply restricted the use of heavy weapons such as artillery or bombing. To fire artillery into Panama City, commanders had to obtain the approval of a two-star commander. Bombing required General Stiner's permission.[14]

By 1800 Task Force BAYONET forces had combed the *Comandancia* compound and controlled it completely. With the loss of the *Comandancia*, the PDF could no longer exercise centralized command and control of its forces. For the remainder of D-Day and the next few days, fighting in Panama City would be sporadic as U.S. forces cleaned up pockets of PDF resistance or engaged small groups of armed civilians belonging to the paramilitary Dignity Battalions.[15]

After the paratroopers of the 82d Airborne Division reinforced the Rangers securing Torrijos-Tocumen Airport, three airborne battalions (1–104, 2–504, and 4–325) operating in central Panama as Task Force PACIFIC conducted the last major combat assaults on D-Day at Panama Viejo, Tinajitas, and Fort Cimarron. One battalion made an airmobile assault into Panama Viejo about 0823 and found Landing Zone Bobcat "hot." There, over a hundred troopers of the PDF's 12th Cavalry Squadron and a special antiterrorist unit fought the airborne force for more than three hours.[16]

Meanwhile, south of Panama Viejo, other airborne troops—the ones delayed in North Carolina by the storm—moved toward Tinajitas to engage the two hundred or so troops of the PDF's 1st Infantry Company. Making the assault at about 1050, the paratroopers found few suitable landing areas for their helicopters on the heavily defended hilltop. Apache and Scout helicopters sustained minor damage from small arms ground fire, but no crewmen were seriously injured. The airborne troops finally subdued the defenders at Tinajitas about 1433. About fifteen miles east of Panama City, airborne troops made nearly unopposed helicopter landings at Fort Cimarron. Except for a small skirmish at the Pecora River Bridge, most of the elite Battalion 2000 broke contact and withdrew. In the three assaults that day the men of Task Force PACIFIC had killed 5, wounded 22, and captured nearly 600 members of the PDF.[17]

In an appraisal of the action on D-Day, General Stiner made several observations about the PDF resistance. Despite radio broadcasts and the use of F-117As and other weapons to stun and intimidate them, most PDF units fought harder than expected before surrendering or fleeing. In conventional fighting, 53 were killed, 55 wounded, and 1,236 soldiers captured. Instead of capitulating at the first sight of U.S. forces and U.S. firepower, they fought for hours and killed 19 U.S. servicemen and wounded 99. Stiner attributed the PDF's willingness to fight to Noriega and the Legislative Assembly's stirring them up with talk of war on 15 December and to possible breaches of U.S. operational security in the wake of the massive airlift from the U.S.[18]

Stiner's troops had prevailed at Colón, Rio Hato, Panama City over the largest concentrations of PDF troops. Because many had dispersed rather than surrender, General Stiner expected that the PDF would continue to resist using hit and run operations, sniping, and sabotage. In Panama City, an estimated three hundred PDF troops had already gathered to operate as well-armed roving bands. A large number of Dignity Battalion members were also active in the city, but they seemed intent on looting and intimidating the citizens rather than fighting the *Yanquis*.[19]

Explanation and Justification

While U.S. forces fought in Panama, the Bush administration prepared to explain JUST CAUSE to the American people. The Policy Coordinating Committee (PCC) of the National Security Council laid the groundwork. Committee members included Brigadier General David C. Meade of J-5; Bernard Aronson, State Department; Richard Brown, OSD; and William Price, NSC. Having learned only hours before of the decision to execute JUST CAUSE, the PCC members worked in the White House Situation Room during the evening of 19 December and the early morning of 20 December. They drafted talking papers for the President and the Secretary of State to use in briefing congressional leaders and answering press questions. They also helped prepare the speech that the President would deliver on national television later that morning.[20]

At 0700 President Bush spoke to the nation:

> Fellow citizens, last night I ordered U.S. military forces to Panama....For nearly two years the United States, nations of Latin America and the Caribbean have worked together to resolve the crisis in Panama. The goals of the United States have been to safeguard the lives of Americans, to defend democracy in Panama, to combat drug trafficking, and to protect the integrity of the Panama Canal Treaty. Many attempts have been made to resolve the crisis through diplomacy and negotiations. All were rejected by the dictator of Panama, General Manuel A. Noriega, an indicted drug trafficker.
>
> Last Friday Noriega declared his military dictatorship to be in a state of war with the United States and publicly threatened the lives of Americans in Panama. The very next day forces under his command shot and killed an unarmed American serviceman, wounded another, arrested

and brutally beat a third American serviceman and then brutally interrogated his wife, threatening her with sexual abuse. That was enough.

General Noriega's reckless threats and attacks upon Americans created an imminent danger to the thirty-five thousand American citizens in Panama. As President I have no higher obligation than to safeguard the lives of American citizens. And that is why I directed our armed forces to protect the lives of Americans citizens in Panama and to bring General Noriega to justice in the United States....

I took this action only after reaching the conclusion that every other avenue was closed and the lives of American citizens were in grave danger....[21]

In an interview with the *New York Times,* Secretary of State Baker discussed the legal justification for U.S. intervention in Panama. Both Article 51 of the United Nations Charter and Article 21 of the Organization of American States Charter recognized the right of self defense that entitled the United States to take appropriate measures to defend U.S. military personnel, U.S. nationals, and U.S. installations. Not only had Panama declared the existence of a state of war and brutalized U.S. citizens, but reports indicated that Noriega supporters were preparing to attack U.S. citizens in residential neighborhoods. Furthermore, the United States had the right and duty under Article IV of the Panama Canal Treaty to protect and defend that strategically important waterway. Finally, the elected government of Endara, Arias Calderón, and Ford welcomed the U.S..[22]

Within the Pentagon Secretary Cheney quietly circulated another legal justification for JUST CAUSE. The *Posse Comitatus* Act (18 U.S.C. 1385) and related legislation (Section 375 of Title 10 of the United States Code) prohibited the use of federal military forces to enforce civilian laws. The Department of Defense included that prohibition as paragraph A.3, Enclosure 4, of DOD Directive 5525.5. According to the Department of Justice, the restriction did not necessarily prevent federal military forces from helping to enforce U.S. laws outside the territorial boundaries of the United States.[23] Hence, on 20 December Cheney approved modification of DOD Directive 5525.5 to state: "With regard to military actions outside the territorial jurisdiction of the United States, however, the Secretary of Defense or the Deputy Secretary of Defense will consider for approval, on a case by case basis, requests for exceptions to the policy restrictions against direct assistance by military personnel to execute the laws. Such requests for exceptions to policy outside the territorial jurisdiction of the United

States should be made only when there are compelling and extraordinary circumstances to justify them."[24] Secretary Cheney issued a memo making JUST CAUSE such an exception: "Consistent with...Revised DOD Directive 5525.5...I approve assistance by the United States Armed Forces in the apprehension of Manuel Noriega of Panama." This action authorized the use of federal troops to assist U.S. law enforcement officers in apprehending Noriega who was under federal indictment for alleged drug trafficking offenses.[25]

Chapter 5

Issues in the National Military Command Center:
Civil Affairs Reservists, the Media Pool,
and U.S. Hostages

Inside the National Military Command Center

On the evening of 19 December, Secretary Cheney slept in his Pentagon suite. Just before H-Hour, he woke and walked to the National Military Command Center (NMCC) to join General Powell and General Kelly as they monitored the assaults in Panama. From that time Secretary Cheney routinely observed the interplay between the events in Panama and General Powell's actions. Periodically, Cheney talked with the President and his advisers in the White House Situation Room. General Powell talked to General Thurman four or five times a day, and General Kelly and Admiral Sheafer spoke with their counterparts at SOUTHCOM dozens of times a day.[1]

At 2000 on 19 December, General Kelly formed a Crisis Action Team (CAT) from the existing J-3 Panama Response Cell and moved it into the NMCC. In accordance with the JCS crisis staffing procedures, Kelly became chief of the CAT. He appointed two vice chiefs, two team chiefs, two deputy team chiefs, and twenty-four representatives from the Joint Staff, the services, and key defense agencies—thirty-one officers divided into Team A working from 0500 to 1700 and Team B working the next twelve hours. For his vice chiefs, Kelly picked Navy Rear Admiral Joseph T. Lopez, the Deputy Director for Current Operations, and Air Force Brigadier General James W. Meier, Deputy Director of the NMCC.[2]

General Kelly activated the CAT to coordinate national support and guidance for USCINCSO and to respond to operational and politico-military issues as they arose. It produced memos, briefing sheets, background papers, and chronologies, and coordinated them with SOUTHCOM and the services. Following staffing and, when appropriate, briefing Secretary Cheney, the CAT would draft messages executing the responses the Chairman or General Kelly selected.[3]

The recent physical reorganization of space within the National Military Command Center greatly facilitated the work of the Crisis Action Team. General Kelly and Admiral Sheafer had spent $4 million to create a Crisis Management Room in which a DIA intelligence task force worked side by side with the CAT. The operations and intelligence officers passed their assessments to the decisionmakers in the nearby Current Situation Room.[4]

General Kelly and Admiral Sheafer had also prepared a room equipped with teleconferencing equipment known as the CJCS-J-3 Conference Room. Starting on D-Day, General Herres; the Director of the Joint Staff, Air Force Lieutenant General Michael P. C. Carns; and Brigadier General Meade, occupied that room. These officers met daily with the National Security Council and the State Department regarding developments relative to JUST CAUSE. Whenever they learned information of operational value, General Meade or another officer briefed the decisionmakers in the Situation Room. Conversely, whenever Secretary Cheney, General Powell, or General Kelly needed clarification of intelligence or politico-military issues, General Herres and his subordinates would query the National Security Council or the State Department.[5]

In the Crisis Management Room, the CAT sent and received operational message traffic. At 1412, on 20 December, special Pro Rata controls over messages concerning ongoing operations and logistical movements were removed, and such messages were placed in routine general service channels. However, certain operational traffic continued to receive Pro Rata protection.[6] As the initial assaults took place, the CAT focused on three issues that would increasingly occupy General Powell's and General Kelly's time—the call-up of civil affairs reservists for duty in Panama, problems of the media pool, and the taking of U.S. hostages.

Civil Affairs

Early on 20 December, General Thurman told General Powell that "no civil affairs units from active or reserve components are available in the theater to support my mission requirements." The Director of the Joint Staff noted that 120 troops from the 96th Civil Affairs Battalion, Fort Bragg, were preparing to depart for Panama. Thurman recommended the call-up of all five reserve civil affairs units to assemble nearly six hundred active and reserve civil affairs troops. Carns agreed on the eventual need for such augmentation.[7]

About 1555, General Thurman began execution of BLIND LOGIC, the civil-military operations plan. JUST CAUSE had largely neutralized the PDF as a military structure and as a police force. In the face of extensive looting and violence in downtown Panama City, Thurman predicted a complete breakdown in law, order, and public safety unless he took immediate action. As soon as the Endara government could provide Panamanian personnel, they would be integrated into the operation. Because remnants of the PDF and the Dignity Battalions were instigating much of the lawlessness, General Thurman asked that troops executing BLIND LOGIC be authorized to use the rules of engagement in effect for JUST CAUSE.[8]

The Media Pool

President Bush had approved use of a DOD-organized media pool—made up either of Washington reporters or those already in Panama—to cover the execution of JUST CAUSE. General Kelly preferred selecting reporters already in Panama, because they represented a smaller security risk before H-Hour. Secretary Cheney believed that the reporters should be the most experienced journalists on Central American affairs, many of whom worked in the Washington area; he chose a Washington-based pool.[9] Cheney delayed media pool activation until after the airlift was well under way. On 18 December, he had heard a weather report that snow or ice on 19 December might delay the airlift for twenty-four hours. Such a delay might tempt a member of the pool to leak the story to a newspaper or television network. Consequently, the Secretary postponed activation of the media pool until after the seven o'clock evening news on 19 December: "I really felt [that] it was a direct trade off between maintaining security of the operation and protecting lives...versus accommodating the press.... Protecting the security of the troops was my first priority."[10]

Activation of the media pool occurred at 1930 on 19 December, but its flight from Andrews Air Force Base, Maryland, took off four hours later. They would not arrive in Panama until nearly four and one half hours after H-Hour. The pool comprised fourteen reporters, most of whom the Secretary of Defense later characterized as comparative novices rather than the experts he had anticipated. They were accompanied by two technicians and three officers acting as escorts.[11] At 2328 on 19 December and 0137 on 20 December, Cheney sent guidance to Thurman on accommodating the newsmen: deploy them with U.S. forces to cover segments of operations. Reassemble them periodically to file their stories in a timely manner, but no sooner than two hours after the commencement of the action being covered. Allow the media temporary access to U.S. communications satellites and uplink equipment until their own equipment arrives. Develop a plan to facilitate arrival of the latter.[12]

At first, the problems of the media pool seemed manageable. Cheney's delayed notification had kept the fourteen reporters from reaching Panama until the troops were wrapping up their initial operations. Helicopters ferried reporters from Fort Clayton to inspect the sites of recent battles at Fort Amador, Torrijos-Tocumen Airport, Punta Paitilla Airfield, Balboa, and the *Comandancia*. To answer media queries, SOUTHCOM had set up a Joint Information Bureau at the Quarry Heights Officers' Club.[13]

From the reporters' point of view, visits to lukewarm battlefields and handouts from public affairs officers failed to meet their basic needs—to travel to active battle sites, observe the action, and then return at once to urban facilities where they could file their stories in time for the next day's news. When reporters requested transportation to ongoing operations, they lost helicopter spaces to troops directly involved in the operation. Over the next two days the arrival of more reporters exacerbated the competition for helicopter seats.[14].

Later Secretary Cheney, General Powell, and General Kelly would agree that more could have been done to facilitate the work of the media pool. Kelly contended that, instead of assigning only three escort officers, the Defense Department should have provided the pool with a team of six to ten officers, experienced in combat and trained in journalism. More escorts could have facilitated media movement with minimal distraction to the combat commander. For maximum effectiveness, escorts and the pool would have to be equipped with dedicated helicopters and crews.[15]

On 20 March, Mr. Fred Hoffman would submit a report to Assistant Secretary of Defense for Public Affairs Pete Williams, which set forth his observations on the problems encountered by the media pool during the deployment to Panama and while covering operations in country. Hoffman concluded with seventeen specific recommendations. The most significant were: at the outset of an operation, the Secretary of Defense should make clear his policy that the media pool must be given every assistance to report on combat operations; the Chairman of the Joint Chiefs of Staff should send a similar message to all echelons in the operational chain of command. All operational plans should contain an annex spelling out how the pool would accompany the lead combat elements. The Assistant Secretary of Defense for Public Affairs should be prepared to apprise the Chairman, his operations deputy, and other senior officers of any obstacles to the pool's accomplishment of its mission. Pool escorts should be experienced combat officers drawn from the services primarily involved in the operation, and officer escorts should deploy in appropriate field uniforms or draw them immediately upon arrival in the area of operations. Public affairs officers from unified commands should meet periodically with reporters and photographers assigned to the pool with whom they might have to work during future operations.[16]

The Hostage Issue

A hostage crisis promised to be a more sensitive issue than either problems with the media pool or civil affairs reservists. Throughout the morning and afternoon of 20 December, three hostage incidents caused concern in the Current Situation Room. About 0249, a CBS executive, John Meyersohn, and an employee of the GTE Corporation, Douglas Miller, were abducted from the Mariott Hotel in Panama City and taken to a PDF site at Rio Abajo. Later, PDF troops abducted eleven employees of the Smithsonian Institution from an island near Colón where they had been engaged in research. From about 1035 to 1500, the Crisis Action Team received reports that the Dignity Battalions were searching the Marriott Hotel for up to thirty U.S. citizens believed to be living there.[17]

General Thurman sent a message to the CAT at 1500 listing his priorities for the remainder of that day: first, ensure that Task Force PACIFIC completed operations at Tinajitas and Fort Cimarron; second, provide President Endara a building where he could safely set up his administration; third, send troops to secure the Marriott Hotel. After an Eastern Airlines pilot and reporters hiding in the Marriott had sent out word of their plight, the press in Washington urged the President to send troops to the rescue.[18]

Secretary Cheney informed General Powell of the President's concern about a developing hostage situation at the Marriott. Ordinarily, General Powell would have let General Thurman run the operation according to his own priorities. As soon as General Stiner's troops had taken Tinajitas and Fort Cimarron, General Powell made a series of calls to General Thurman concerning the need to occupy the Marriott as soon as possible. At one point General Powell said. "You've got to have a plan. Tell me when it's [the Marriott Hotel] going to be taken."[19]

General Thurman replied at 1620 that General Stiner would need about four hours to complete preparations for the operation. Not satisfied, General Powell directed Thurman to have Stiner's troops enter the Marriott no later than midnight. Powell also wanted Stiner to stop pro-Noriega broadcasts at Radio Nacional and to establish the Endara government with all haste. By 2138 troops of the 82d Airborne Division had cleared the Marriott Hotel. The Americans there came out of hiding and greeted their rescuers.[20]

Chapter 6

Last Combat, Civil Affairs,
and the Hunt for Noriega
21–24 December 1989

Last Combat with the PDF

Late in the evening of 20 December, a composite brigade of the 7th Infantry Division (L) and the 16th Military Police Brigade arrived in Panama. Their arrival reflected the changing situation. Regular combat with PDF units wound down during the next four days, but the need to deal with remnants of the PDF and to conduct civil-military operations increased. Taking command of Task Force ATLANTIC, the brigade of the 7th Infantry Division (L) conducted stabilization operations while the military police assisted civil affairs operations primarily in the cities.[1]

Stabilization operations took place from the periphery of Panama City to Darien Province. These operations combined Rangers and regular troops. At night, Rangers or other special operations forces contacted the PDF commanders and urged them to surrender by daybreak; meanwhile, conventional forces surrounded the target area. At dawn, if the PDF troops refused to surrender, the conventional forces feigned an attack or launched a mild attack. Usually the PDF troops surrendered quickly.[2]

On Friday, 22 December 1989, President Endara abolished the PDF and reorganized a portion of it as the cadre for the new *Fuerza_Publica* (Public Force). President Endara appointed the former chief of the Panamanian navy, Roberto Armijo, to lead the new force. Noriega supporters fought on in the hope that Noriega might reappear to lead them. In the cities and larger towns west of Panama City, PDF remnants and Dignity Battalions sporadically challenged U.S. troops and military police trying to restore law and order.[3]

As Endara abolished the PDF, a force of Rangers moved north of Rio Hato to capture PDF elements at Penonome in Cocle Province. Another force moved to neutralize two platoons of the PDF's 5th Rifle Company believed to be holding out at La Chorrera, a small town about fifteen miles southwest of Panama City. Meanwhile, General Stiner prepared to conduct major assaults in the distant provinces of Chiriqui and Bocas del Toro near Costa Rica and the province of Darien near Colombia. To support Stiner, General Thurman asked General Powell for a second brigade of the 7th Infantry Division (L). Secretary Cheney ordered the deployment.[4]

U.S. forces suffered a minor setback. On Saturday, 23 December, a group of about thirty Dignity Battalion members approached a unit of 3–504 Airborne guarding the Madden Dam. They carried a white flag, but, as the U.S. paratroopers stepped from cover to accept their weapons, the Panamanians suddenly opened fire. The surprised paratroopers had nineteen wounded, but drove off the irregulars killing at least five of them.[5]

The relatively few casualties were quickly returned to the United States. By 21 December General Thurman's staff reported 19 killed, 117 wounded, and 1 missing. Evacuation of the wounded, to Kelly Air Force Base, Texas, began with the first C-141 carrying forty-three wounded out of Panama on D-Day; smaller evacuation flights followed during the next three days. Dead servicemen were flown to Dover Air Force Base, Delaware.[6]

The eleven Smithsonian employees abducted on D-Day were located on 22 December. Deserted by their captors and unharmed, they were evacuated to Fort Clayton. Meanwhile, reports of U.S. employees of the Evergreen Company and other U.S. citizens being held hostage proved to be false. Those citizens believed to be in genuine danger were moved to nearby U.S. military installations. During this period, U.S. forces continued to look for the CBS executive, John Meyersohn, and the GTE employee, Douglas Miller, both of whom were being held hostage at Rio Abajo.[7]

With the PDF in disarray and largely on the run after D-Day, members of the paramilitary Dignity Battalions constituted the chief danger to U.S. troops and U.S. civilians. Reportedly under the command of Benjamin Colomarco, squad-sized groups in Panama City and other urban areas looted stores and robbed private residences in upper class neighborhoods. Starting on 21 December, in Panama City, these irregulars began sniping at the U.S. embassy. For the next few days sniping and standoff attacks by the Dignity Battalions impeded efforts to establish order.

Civil Affairs and PROMOTE LIBERTY

Looting compelled General Thurman to begin the civil affairs operation BLIND LOGIC on 20 December. At 0953 on 21 December, General Powell told Thurman that the National Command Authorities had formally approved the plan's execution, including deployment of nearly three hundred civil affairs reservists. General Thurman created a civil-military operations task force combining some of his own troops with those of the 96th Civil Affairs Battalion, expected to arrive on 22 December, and three hundred reservists who would follow over the next three weeks.[8]

Kelly and his staff agreed that BLIND LOGIC made a poor name for an operation requiring great skill and high purpose. They renamed the civil affairs operation PROMOTE LIBERTY. The first stage of PROMOTE LIBERTY concentrated on public safety, health, and population control measures. Later, the U.S. country team and the new Panamanian government took responsibility for population control, rebuilding commerce, winning the support of the people for reforms, and restructuring the PDF into separate police, customs, and defense organizations. The commander of the 96th Civil Affairs Battalion would assign civil affairs forces to Zone P (Panama City and the eastern provinces), Zone C (Colón), and Zone D (the provinces west of Panama City).[9]

On 22 December, the 96th Civil Affairs Battalion landed in Panama. General Hartzog greeted the commander with an extensive list of tasks: restore basic functions throughout Panama City, establish a police force, provide emergency food distribution, create a night watch using helicopters with spotlights, protect property, supervise Panamanian contractors in cleaning up the city, restore the production and distribution of newspapers, and develop a grassroots organization to "sell" the Endara government to the public. In one of his first moves, the commander of the civil-military operations task force worked with Colonel Roberto Armijo of the new *Fuerza Publica* to recruit volunteers for police duty. Of the four hundred volunteers, mostly former policemen or soldiers under the PDF, only 160 were found acceptable.[10]

The Dignity Battalions and other PDF remnants continued to resist. On Saturday, 23 December, the Deputy Chief of Mission, John Bushnell, reported that shooting incidents at the U.S. embassy continued. Assailants had fired nearly seventy shots into his car; miraculously only one hit the diplomat's flak jacket. Bushnell attributed the vigor of the resistance to fear of Noriega and the expectation that he would soon receive help from Cuba and Nicaragua. He asked General Stiner for more troops to pacify Panama City. Stiner promised help, but could not concentrate all his forces in Panama City while Noriega remained free to rally PDF holdouts in the provinces.[11]

Meanwhile, General Powell and General Kelly talked with General Thurman about a two-pronged psychological warfare campaign to win public support for Endara and to persuade resisters to lay down their arms. The psychological operations specialists deployed to Panama for JUST CAUSE would join General Thurman's forces in putting forth themes including: U.S. troops had deployed to protect the lives and property of U.S. citizens; U.S. troops would help President Endara form a government responsive to the will and aspirations of the people; U.S. differences were with Noriega, not with the Panamanian people; U.S. forces would depart as soon as the new government could take over; the United States would reward those assisting in locating PDF leaders and weapons caches; and a reward of $1 million would be paid for anyone apprehending Noriega and turning him over to U.S. forces.[12]

Sporadic fighting and looting continued in Panama City. On 24 December, SOUTHCOM intelligence estimated that from two hundred to five hundred resisters still operated in the capital. Thurman's headquarters picked up a rumor that the Dignity Battalions were preparing a six-company attack against U.S. troops at Punta Paitilla on Christmas Day. General Thurman hoped they would attempt such an action and come into the open where superior U.S. firepower and skill would "destroy them as a credible threat." Thurman considered the Dignity Battalions a serious threat throughout the country. Since JUST CAUSE began, his analysts increased to eighteen the number of Dignity Battalions believed in existence and connected by a simple, functional system of radio repeaters.[13]

Neither General Kelly nor General Thurman's top operations officers expected the Dignity Battalions to concentrate their forces for a conventional assault; they expected guerrilla warfare. Kelly and General Hartzog agreed on 24 December to help Colonel Armijo expand the number of police in the *Fuerza Publica* as it was the quickest way to regain order in the cities. To pacify the countryside, Major General William K. James, Deputy USCINCSO, called the Crisis Action Team to recommend deployment from Fort Bragg of a U.S. Special Forces battalion or even a Special Forces Group. Special Forces teams would train and advise Panamanian police in liberated areas outside the major cities. In the opinion of General James, this would expedite the withdrawal of U.S. combat troops.[14]

The Hunt for Noriega

The hunt for Noriega began when special operations teams and paratroopers landed on D-Day. It continued for four days. On 21 December, General Thurman made the capture of the Panamanian dictator his second highest priority after the neutralization of the PDF. Noriega was mainly a symbol of resistance rather than a military threat. Continued resistance by Noriega supporters would occupy large numbers of U.S. forces in Panama. A prolonged presence of these forces could raise Latin American concern about U.S. violation of the sovereign rights of a Latin American state.

A lengthy U.S. military presence could also undermine the legitimacy of the Endara government. According to the experts in J-5 and the Deputies Committee of the National Security Council, Latin American recognition of the Endara government hinged upon Endara's ability to demonstrate that he could restore law and order without U.S. combat troops. With Noriega captured or killed, resistance to Endara was expected to diminish to the point where the *Fuerza Publica* could function effectively with little or no help from U.S. troops.[15]

On 21 December, General Kelly called General Hartzog; they discussed a bounty on Noriega to speed his capture. A reward of $1 million would later be approved, but even before it was announced individuals reported sighting Noriega and his cronies. Teams investigating the sites found them empty. In at least two cases, evidence indicated that Noriega or his supporters had just fled in a frantic game of hide and seek with their pursuers.[16]

On 22 December, Task Force BAYONET personnel searched Noriega's residence at Fort Amador. They found fifty kilograms of white powder initially believed to be cocaine, but later identified as a cooking ingredient. They also found pictures of Hitler, an extensive pornography collection, $83,000 in cash, and a "witches diary," chronicling visits by two witches from Brazil who periodically flew to Panama to provide Noriega with opportunities to practice black magic. Later that day, special operations forces searched another Noriega residence where they discovered approximately $8 million and a valuable art collection. They also found a briefcase containing lists of bank accounts in Switzerland and the Cayman Islands, $200,000 in cash, a personal wallet, bifocals, and three diplomatic passports.[17]

On the evening of 22 December, General Thurman speculated that Noriega was hiding in Panama City, or, more likely, heading west to his home province of Chiriqui. Reports received the next day supported the latter possibility. Intelligence analysts speculated that Noriega might execute PLANAMONTANA, a contingency plan for setting up a guerrilla base in the mountains; Noriega could then orchestrate raids and terrorism against U.S. forces and the Endara government.[18]

On 24 December, plans for the last major combat assault of JUST CAUSE, the taking of David (the provincial capital of Chiriqui Province) and the headquarters for the PDF's 5th Military Zone, were completed. Generals Thurman and Stiner believed that the surrender of the zone headquarters and search operations into the mountainous countryside would thwart PLANAMONTANA. At David, a PDF captain named Jurado contacted General Cisneros and offered to surrender the zone headquarters and turn over its commander, Lieutenant Colonel Luis Del Cid. In case Jurado's offer failed to materialize, General Thurman insisted on deploying the assault force and supporting battalion as planned. Secretary Cheney approved execution of the operation for Christmas Day.[19]

Noriega once again did the unexpected. Instead of staging a last ditch fight in the hills of Chiriqui, he sought refuge in the embassy of the papal nuncio, Monsignor José Sebastían Laboa. Monsignor Laboa had granted Noriega's political adversary, Endara, sanctuary in the *Nunciatura* after the election of May 1989. General Thurman and General Stiner had anticipated the possibility that Noriega might seek asylum in the embassy of a sympathetic country. Stiner's troops had cordoned off the embassies of Cuba, Nicaragua, and Libya and kept several other embassies under surveillance. Probably aware that no U.S. troops watched the *Nunciatura*, Noriega contacted Monsignor Laboa on 24 December and requested political asylum until he could obtain entry into Cuba or Spain.[20]

Desiring to end the bloodshed, Monsignor Laboa agreed to give Noriega temporary political refuge until he could be moved out of Panama to a third country. At about 1445 on 24 December, the nuncio sent an official car to meet Noriega at a secret rendezvous and bring him to the *Nunciatura*. Later, Laboa permitted some of Noriega's chief advisers to join him, including Lieutenant Colonel Nivaldo Madrinan, Chief of Noriega's Department of National Investigation; Captain Asuncion Gaitan, Noriega's senior aide and chief of security; Colonel Arnulfo Castrejon, commander of the navy; Lieutenant Colonel Carlos Velarde, a military chaplain; and Captain Ivan Castillo, Noriega's personal bodyguard, with his wife. In addition to this group, the nuncio had earlier granted asylum to eight civilians and five Basque separatists.[21]

Chapter 7

The *Nunciatura*
24 December 1989–3 January 1990

An Overview

At about 1500 on 24 December, General Thurman learned of Noriega's presence in the *Nunciatura* and sent troops from Task Force GREEN and the military police brigade to cordon off the diplomatic compound. Thurman notified General Kelly at about 1600 that Noriega was trapped, yet, for the time being, safe from U.S. apprehension. Surprised and elated, Secretary Cheney told General Powell, "Don't let that guy out of the compound." The State Department immediately informed the Vatican of the situation and requested that it deny Noriega asylum. Since most of the Vatican dignitaries were about to celebrate Midnight Mass at St. Peter's, no response was made that day.[1]

Daily, from Christmas Eve to 3 January 1990, efforts to secure Noriega's release from the *Nunciatura* occupied civilian and military leaders. Secretary of State Baker communicated through the papal nuncio, Archbishop Pio Laghi, to the papal Secretary of State, Cardinal Angelo Sodano. The results of these communications passed through the White House Situation Room to the National Military Command Center, which kept Secretary Cheney, General Powell and General Kelly posted. Powell and Kelly informed General Thurman of developments and reported his assessments to the White House. In Panama, Major General Cisneros negotiated with Monsignor Laboa, occasionally outside the gate of the *Nunciatura*.[2]

General Powell spoke several times each day to General Thurman, giving him what Powell referred to as "the view from the 32d floor." During those conversations Powell told Thurman of the White House concerns and State Department negotiations with the Vatican. Thurman briefed Powell on operational needs and the status of Cisneros's talks with Monsignor Laboa. Far more frequently, General Kelly and the Crisis Action Team communicated with General Hartzog and his staff on the details of reporting and implementing decisions made by their superiors.[3]

The day that Noriega retreated to the *Nunciatura*, General Herres reached agreement with Mr. Robin Ross, the chief of staff to Attorney General Richard Thornburgh, that the Drug Enforcement Administration (DEA) would be the civilian agency to take custody of Noriega once apprehended. In Panama, General Stiner's forces would provide Noriega and his DEA escort protection and transportation for Noriega's extradition to the jurisdiction of the federal district court in Miami. However, for the next ten days, General Powell, General Thurman, and their staffs would be increasingly preoccupied with problems including rules of engagement for cordoning off the *Nunciatura*, the negative impact of rock music played there, contretemps with Cuban and Nicaraguan diplomats, and, above all, Vatican resistance to U.S. requests for custody of Noriega.[4]

Rules of Engagement for Cordoning Off the *Nunciatura*

The presence of Noriega and some of his top aides at the *Nunciatura* presented General Thurman with two problems—first a security problem and, later, a potential hostage situation. From the *Nunciatura* Noriega could use couriers to perpetuate and coordinate resistance by his followers on the outside. In addition to using visitors posing as diplomats or negotiators to smuggle communications back and forth, he might even attempt to escape by hiding in a visitor's vehicle as it left the compound. Responding to such concerns, on 24 December, General Kelly told General Hartzog that troops could stop diplomatic cars entering or departing the *Nunciatura* and demand identification. If suspicion existed that Noriega or one of his lieutenants might be hiding in the trunk of a car, it could be searched, preferably in the presence of representatives of the Endara government. If Noriega or his lieutenants were found during such a search, they should be placed in U.S. military custody pending further instructions.[5]

At 1714 on 24 December, the Acting Secretary of State, Robert Kimmett, insisted on making some exceptions. Kimmett instructed the Deputy Chief of Mission, John Bushnell, to allow unhindered access to and from the *Nunciatura* to all Vatican diplomats and to the top four officials of the new Panamanian government—Endara, Arias Calderón, Ford, and the Foreign Minister. Kimmett added that, wherever possible, it would be "preferable" for Bushnell to notify General Thurman in advance of such visits. General Thurman complained that the word preferable opened a huge loophole, so he requested that advance notice be given for all visits to the *Nunciatura*. General Powell supported Thurman's request, and on 26 December, the Deputies Committee of the National Security Council approved it. They did, however, allow Bushnell to authorize visits for other Panamanians, provided that he notified Thurman's headquarters in advance.[6]

As soon as Washington authorities resolved the question of visitor control, the potential for a hostage situation at the *Nunciatura* demanded additional guidance. On 26 December, Monsignor Laboa informed General Stiner that, should Noriega and his men use their weapons to take control of the *Nunciatura*, Laboa would approve entry of Stiner's troops into the compound. After being briefed by General Powell, Secretary Cheney gave permission for U.S. troops to enter the *Nunciatura*, but only after Stiner's men heard shots fired within.[7]

On 27 December, General Kelly briefed Acting Secretary of Defense Donald Atwood on General Thurman's request to employ military snipers should a hostage situation erupt at the *Nunciatura*. Atwood answered: "You are authorized to use the appropriate military force necessary to resolve any hostage situation...which you have reason to believe is immediately life threatening. Of course, if time permits, you are expected to consult with the National Command Authorities." Meeting with General Kelly on 31 December, Secretary Atwood affirmed his earlier guidance. He further stipulated that the entry of U.S. troops into the *Nunciatura* must be requested directly by the Vatican, not Laboa; after the entry, the Vatican must publicly acknowledge that it had made the request.[8]

Rock Music at the *Nunciatura*

In addition to the cordon of troops, General Stiner erected a sound barrier around the *Nunciatura* in the wake of a visit there on Christmas Day by General Thurman. On Christmas morning, Thurman spoke personally to Monsignor Laboa at the gate of the *Nunciatura*. As Thurman turned to depart, a reporter from an upper floor window of the nearby Holiday Inn shouted, "Hey General Thurman, how ya doin'? Merry Christmas!" Fearing that reporters could use powerful microphones to eavesdrop on delicate negotiations between Cisneros and Laboa, General Thurman ordered that a music barrier be set up around the *Nunciatura*. Later, as hard rock music blared around the clock, a psychological operations specialist claimed it was part of a campaign to harass Noriega.[9]

Depicted as a form of press censorship by the media, the rock music soon aroused other critics. By 28 December, diplomats, Catholics in the United States, and Vatican officials had deplored the practice as a clumsy effort to harass Noriega that inflicted needless stress upon the papal nuncio and his staff. The President made his concern known to Secretary Cheney and General Powell.[10]

About 1140 General Powell asked Brigadier General Meier to explain the purpose of the music. Meier repeated General Thurman's original rationale: to mask sensitive negotiations between General Cisneros and Monsignor Laboa. General Thurman, however, also justified the music as an effective psychological tool. At this point,

Laboa was talking about sleeping outside the compound, and Noriega and his henchmen were becoming increasingly worried and nervous. Thurman believed that applying pressure, not only to Noriega but to his host as well, would compel Monsignor Laboa to release Noriega.[11]

In the face of mounting public criticism and presidential concern, General Powell grew increasingly uncomfortable with the rock music at the *Nunciatura*. President Bush viewed the tactic as politically embarrassing and "irritating and petty." On 29 December, after returning from an NSC meeting in which he had been instructed not to "make things any more difficult or unpleasant for Monsignor Laboa than necessary," Powell told Thurman to stop the music. Rear Admiral Sheafer relayed the order to Thurman's staff and tasked the National Security Agency to provide a less provocative noise jammer to prevent the media from eavesdropping on negotiations between Cisneros and Laboa.[12]

Contretemps over Cuban and Nicaraguan Diplomatic Privileges

On 28 December, a confrontation between U.S. troops and Cuban diplomats at the Cuban ambassador's residence promised embarrassment. At 1530 the Cuban ambassador to Panama, Lazaro Mora, and his escort, Alberto Cabrera, tried to depart Mora's residence. Members of the 82d Airborne Division, in a cordon around the residence, stopped the two men and asked for credentials. Cabrera's papers identified him as the Cuban embassy's First Secretary for Exterior Affairs, but the JTFPM Black List described Cabrera as a hostile intelligence officer to be detained. Amidst vociferous protests by the two Cubans, the troopers sought instructions. Brigade headquarters ordered them to bring Cabrera to Panama Viejo, the headquarters of Joint Task Force South. The Cuban ambassador insisted on accompanying Cabrera.[13]

To avert an international incident, General Stiner returned the two Cubans to Mora's residence by 1700. Stiner explained that in using the black list the troopers had carried out standard procedure for locating members of the PDF wanted on criminal charges in the United States; he assured General Kelly that both diplomats had been treated with respect and dignity. When the Cuban government protested the incident, the State Department denied that there had been any arrests or abuse and assured Cuban officials that the troops had acted reasonably under the circumstances.[14]

On 29 December, U.S. troops in the El Dorado section of Panama City forced their way into what would later be identified as the residence of the Nicaraguan ambassador, Alberto Feero. Early on 29 December, a

U.S. citizen, who had provided reliable tips in the past, told General Stiner's staff that they could find a cache of weapons and a supply of drugs at the residence. At 1630 troops surrounded the house, gave two orders to come out, and then fired two bursts of rifle fire as a warning. The occupants came out. At that time Feero appeared, claimed to be the Nicaraguan ambassador and demanded that the troops leave. Neither Feero nor the other occupants produced papers proving their claim.[15] An official-looking seal (General Powell later said it was the size of a manhole cover) on the outside of the building indicated that the house was affiliated with the Nicaraguan embassy. Uncertain whether to search the premises, the unit commander called for instructions. A liaison officer from the U.S. embassy informed JTFSO headquarters that his list showed no ambassadorial residence in El Dorado, but U.S. embassy clerical personnel had failed to update the list to show that in April 1989 the Nicaraguan ambassador had moved into the residence in question.

Acting on inaccurate information from the U.S. embassy, troops entered the residence at 1900. They found and removed a weapons cache that included 4 Uzi machineguns, 7 rocket-propelled grenade launchers (RPG-7s), 15 T-65 automatic weapons, and 12 AK-47 assault rifles. When the U.S. embassy in Panama City belatedly confirmed the diplomatic status of the residence, the U.S. troops returned the weapons. When Nicaragua protested the U.S. entry as a violation of diplomatic immunity, United States representatives replied that the presence of such weapons violated diplomatic privilege.[16]

Very early on the morning of 30 December, the State Department told the Joint Staff that the government of Nicaragua, in retaliation for the U.S. search of Ambassador Feero's residence, would expel up to forty U.S. embassy workers within the next seventy-two hours. To avert future reprisals, the State Department sent General Thurman detailed guidance later that day on the diplomatic privileges and immunities that his forces must observe under the rules of the Vienna Convention. Article 22 permitted entry and search of an embassy or mission, or search of its property or transportation, only if there existed imminent danger to public safety such as loss of life or bodily injury that could be averted by immediate action. Mere suspicion that weapons were cached on such premises did not provide a basis for entry.[17] Article 38 applied the same standard of inviolability to the private residence of a diplomat. Moreover, if doubt existed on the diplomatic status of the resident, it should be resolved before entry. Article 41 declared that, while it was forbidden for diplomatic missions or residences to contain arms caches, only the host government had the authority either to demand their removal or to close and search the premises. To preclude mistakes, the State Department recommended that U.S. officials work with the

Endara government to update listings and addresses of private diplomatic residences.[18]

Negotiations with the Vatican

During the final days of JUST CAUSE, negotiations with the Vatican for the release of Noriega into U.S. custody increasingly occupied center stage. On Christmas Day, the papal secretary of state responded to Secretary Baker's request for the release of Noriega with a polite but firm refusal. In the Vatican's view, Monsignor Laboa was not granting asylum to a man indicted for international crimes, but giving him "political refuge" to end the bloodshed. The Vatican proposed offering refuge until a third country could be found to grant Noriega permanent asylum. During the next two days Spain, Peru, Mexico, and other countries refused asylum; Cuba's offer of asylum to Noriega, his family, and his lieutenants proved unacceptable to the United States.[19]

After a meeting of the National Security Council on 29 December, General Powell relayed policy guidance to General Thurman to gain custody of Noriega, but to do it in a way that did not rupture relations with the Vatican. Encouraging Panamanian leaders to appeal to the Pope to release Noriega to U.S. officials offered Thurman an indirect but effective way of expediting the negotiations. President Endara had already appealed to Pope John Paul II in a letter explaining that the continued presence of Noriega in Panama fueled pro-Noriega propaganda.[20]

Meanwhile, General Thurman granted Archbishop Marcos McGrath, the senior Catholic prelate in Panama, permission to visit the "witch house" and other Noriega residences to "gain insight into the man's soul." After the tour, Archbishop McGrath convened a conference of Panamanian bishops to discuss what he had learned. On 29 December, the bishops of Panama wrote John Paul II a letter explaining that the dictator had committed torture and murder, had practiced devil worship and voodoo, and had stockpiled weapons and ammunition in preparation for prolonged and bloody guerrilla warfare. They urged the Pope to order his release to U.S. custody.[21]

The indirect approach worked. On 29 December, the Vatican newspaper, *L'Osservatore Romano*, carried a communique stating that the Vatican had never intended to hinder justice by granting Noriega refuge. The Vatican informed Secretary Baker that its senior expert on Central America, Monsignor Giacinto Berlocco, would fly to Panama to help Monsignor Laboa and General Cisneros persuade Noriega to turn himself over to U.S. justice. To assist General Cisneros, Secretary

Baker provided a top diplomat, Deputy Assistant Secretary of State Michael Kozak.[22]

Monsignor Berlocco arrived on 1 January and confided in General Cisneros that he hoped for "a fair, speedy, and just resolution of the problem." The next day, Monsignors Berlocco and Laboa talked with General Cisneros and Mr. Kozak. They discussed an offer from Noriega to surrender on condition that the United States agree not to pursue the death penalty at his trial and that it not extradite him to Panama. Kozak agreed to the first condition, but only promised to "reduce the possibility of his extradition back to Panama."[23]

Reports of a massive anti-Noriega rally near the *Nunciatura*, to take place on the afternoon of 3 January, provided U.S. and Vatican diplomats with the final factor needed to persuade Noriega. General Hartzog informed General Kelly that General Stiner would move extra troops into the area and had arranged overhead surveillance by Air Force AC-130s and Army AH-64s. If shots were fired, Stiner's troops and aircraft would not fire into the crowd, but try to locate and shoot the gunmen. Stiner's precautions succeeded. A crowd of ten thousand people gathered at Balboa and demonstrated peacefully. No shots were fired into or from the crowd.[24]

The angry sounds of the crowd and the echoes of anti-Noriega slogans enabled Monsignor Laboa to make Noriega choose to leave voluntarily, or at noon on 4 January, Laboa would lift diplomatic immunity at the *Nunciatura*. Laboa left open the possibility that, if U.S. troops did not enter, an anti-Noriega crowd might. Noriega agreed to surrender, but requested that the transfer be secret, he be allowed to call his wife at the Cuban embassy, he be given a military uniform to wear, Laboa accompany him to the gate, and he be allowed to talk with General Cisneros.

General Cisneros refused to meet with Noriega. Major General Downing, the Commander of the Joint Special Operations Task Force, conducted the turnover which took place secretly within the span of an hour. At 2045 on 3 January, Monsignor Laboa notified Downing that Noriega was coming out. Three minutes later, Noriega walked through the gate, and U.S. troops handcuffed him. The former strongman balked, but calmed down and walked to the helicopter. At 2053 General Thurman told General Kelly, "He is out of the gate and in the school." On the ramp of a C-130 at Howard Air Force Base, agents from the Drug Enforcement Administration informed Noriega of his rights and arrested him. The C-130 departed Panama for Homestead Air Force Base, Florida, at 2131.

Chapter 8

The End of Organized Resistance,
the Shift to Nationbuilding, and Redeployment
25 December 1989–3 January 1990

Except for the planned assault into Chiriqui Province on Christmas Day, the grant of political refuge to Noriega had signalled the end of JUST CAUSE as a combat operation. Commanders and staffs at the Pentagon and at Quarry Heights now began assessing final casualties; disposing of captured weapons; explaining the details of the operation to Congress and the media; redeploying Rangers, airborne, and special operations forces back to the U.S. and deactivating the Crisis Action Team in the National Military Command Center. In Panama, General Thurman and General Stiner gradually transferred JTFSO assets to the civil affairs operation, PROMOTE LIBERTY.

End of the Fighting

At 1100 on Christmas Day, Rangers made an air assault into David, the last PDF stronghold. Lieutenant Colonel Del Cid, the commander of the 5th Military Zone, and the PDF's 3d Rifle Company surrendered. Wanted by the United States on drug trafficking charges, Del Cid was immediately flown to Howard Air Force Base and handed over to Drug Enforcement Administration officers. The Rangers found two helicopters and an arsenal of seven thousand weapons. Later, the Rangers flew into Boquete, Volcan, La Escondida, and Bocas del Toro; they found several weapons caches. On 26 December, elements of the 82d Airborne Division made an air assault into Flamenco Island where they uncovered weapons caches. The results of previous combat actions and word of Noriega's flight to the *Nunciatura* had ended organized resistance by combat forces. Throughout Panama, members of the PDF waited for the U.S. forces to accept their surrender.[1]

By midnight on 25 December, General Thurman submitted revised casualty figures on JUST CAUSE: 23 U.S. killed and 322 wounded; 297 Panamanians killed, 123 wounded, and 468 detained. Joint Task Force South had captured 36 armored vehicles, 7 boats, 33 aircraft, and 33,507 weapons. By the close of the operation, the number of captured weapons rose to 77,553, of which 8,848 had been turned in for $811,078. A "weapons for dollars program" paid $25 for a hand grenade, $100 for a pistol, $125 for a rifle, $150 for an automatic rifle, and $150 for a mine.[2]

Casualty figures for U.S. forces remained constant, but Panamanian figures fluctuated. By 8 January 1990, the U.S. forces raised the number of Panamanian military dead to 314; the Endara government estimated that 203 civilians died during the fighting. On 21 May 1990, based upon an actual body count, the Panamanian Minister of Health provided new numbers of Panamanians killed during JUST CAUSE: 51 uniformed PDF, 58 unidentified civilians, and 143 identified civilians for a total of 252.[3] General Kelly attributed the higher JTFSO figures to the tendency of combatants firing at the same target to each claim credit for it. But the latest Panamanian estimates overlooked a significant number of dead still to be recovered from the field, and General Kelly believed that the true Panamanian casualty figure lay somewhere between the figures of the JTFSO and the Panamanian ministry.[4]

Civil Affairs and the Question of Redeployment

With Noriega in the *Nunciatura*, PROMOTE LIBERTY began to show growing vitality. On Tuesday, 26 December, 25 civil affairs reservists landed in Panama; 120 more were expected on 1 January and up to 155 more by 15 January. General Thurman asked General Kelly for more U.S. Special Forces to assist the civil affairs troops in reestablishing law and order, promoting stability, and assisting the establishment of the new Panamanian government. From 26 December to 3 January, civil affairs and Special Forces troops helped distribute 1,660 tons of food, mostly "Meals Ready to Eat", and 218 tons of DOD medical supplies. They also organized a camp at Balboa for nearly five thousand persons displaced by the fighting.[5]

Despite the defeat of the PDF, the Dignity Battalions and armed criminal elements continued looting and shooting. General Thurman answered an earlier request from General Powell to submit supplementary rules of engagement. To discourage looters, Thurman recommended allowing the on-scene commander to authorize warning shots as a deterrent; employing minimum force to apprehend looters for turnover to the civilian authorities; and using deadly force only if necessary to save lives. General Thurman recommended more detailed ROE for roadblocks and defensive positions. After establishing clearly marked perimeter limits, troops should be authorized to fire warning shots to deter violators. If warnings failed, minimum force should be used to detain civilian infiltrators. For armed encroachers, troops should be allowed to use whatever force was necessary to disarm and detain them. Troops should also be permitted to disable or attack any vehicle trying to force its way past a checkpoint. Troops should be permitted to use proportional force, up to and including deadly force, to repulse an outright attack or even the threat of an attack. To clear buildings, General Thurman's proposed ROE specified this procedure: warn the occupants to exit the building; if necessary, fire warning shots to hasten their movement; avoid damage to medical, religious, and historical sites unless they are clearly being used for attacks against U.S. troops or against civilians; minimize damage to nonmilitary government buildings and dwellings; and respect private property to the maximum extent possible.[6]

Two days after submission of these proposed additional ROE, General Thurman addressed another key question. When could U.S. combat and logistical troops deployed for JUST CAUSE, but not needed for PROMOTE LIBERTY, return to the United States? Early in the afternoon of Thursday, 28 December, Thurman sent this assessment: Redeployment of the majority of combat forces should begin as soon as possible after removal of Noriega from the *Nunciatura* and final neutralization of the Dignity Battalions. General Thurman concluded that the longer JUST CAUSE forces remained in Panama, especially beyond thirty days, the more difficult it would be "to declare the operation a success." He recommended redeployment first of Rangers and all other special operations forces, then troops of the 82d Airborne Division, and then the Air Force units that supported combat operations. A small residual combat force should be retained indefinitely under the command of Major General Cisneros.[7]

By 1 January, Thurman believed the Dignity Battalions no longer posed a major threat. He revised his assessment and advised General Powell that: "The situation...other than for the apprehension of Noriega...is proceeding according to plan.....It is now possible to begin redeployment of some of our forces by taking advantage of strategic airlift backhaul." Within three to five days, even if Noriega were not captured, General Thurman recommended redeployment of these special operations units: one squadron of Army Special Mission Units, two assault teams from SEAL Team SIX, elements of Task Force 160, and one Ranger battalion. SEAL Team TWO and an aviation squadron from the Army Special Mission Units had left that day.[8] Rear Admiral Lopez responded to General Thurman's recommendations for redeployment. He informed General Hartzog that the Joint Staff would consider sequential redeployment of major units but required specific dates and sizes of the elements to be redeployed.[9]

The need to institute checks and balances within the Panamanian military and security forces worked against rapid withdrawal of U.S. forces. The U.S. ambassador, Arthur H. Davis, wanted U.S. forces to remain on hand to deter any interference with efforts by the Endara government to separate and to "civilianize" the functions once monopolized by the PDF. In a message to Secretary Baker he explained that a new structure should be created before U.S. forces withdrew. So far the leaders of the new *Fuerza Publica* had agreed to separate the investigative police, the immigration service, and the prison police from the armed forces; however, *Fuerza Publica* leaders seemed intent on thwarting further separations by Vice President Arias Calderón.[10]

General Thurman and Ambassador Davis agreed with Arias Calderon's desire to create separate functions from a list that included police, national investigations, customs, prisons, air support, coast guard, presidential security, traffic registration, traffic law enforcement, forest service, counternarcotics, and counterterrorism. They also agreed that the *Fuerza Publica* should rely on U.S. combat forces to defend the Panama Canal from attack. Whatever the ultimate separation of functions, Thurman and Davis favored retention within the *Fuerza Publica* of companies for crowd control and a modest counterinsurgency force to resist Cuban subversion.[11]

General Powell determined that the presence in Panama of nearly seventeen thousand combat troops above the ninety-five hundred troops normally assigned to SOUTHCOM could not continue indefinitely. On 3 January, he approved redeployment of special operations troops and selected items of equipment. Powell also directed General Thurman to use U.S. aircraft between 7 and 26 January to redeploy the 401st Military Police Company (7–10 January), the 82d Airborne Division (10–18 January), the XVIIIth Airborne Corps headquarters and corps troops (12–20 January), an assault helicopter company of the 7th Infantry Division (L) (14–22 January), Air Force forces (AFFOR) (10–26 January), XVIIIth Airborne Corps Support Command (COSCOM) (14–26 January), and the Division Ready Brigade, 7th Infantry Division (L) (18-26 January).[12]

Late in the evening of 3 January 1990, President Bush announced that, with the capture of Noriega, General Stiner's task force had attained all the objectives set for JUST CAUSE. The President continued:

> I want to thank the Vatican and the papal nuncio in Panama for their even-handed, statesmenlike assistance in recent days....The return of General Noriega marks a significant milestone in 'Operation JUST CAUSE.'...The first U.S. combat troops have already been withdrawn from Panama. Others will follow as quickly as the local situation will permit....The armed forces...have performed their mission courageously and effectively, and I again want

to express my gratitude....A free and prosperous Panama will be an enduring tribute.[13]

At noon on 5 January, General Kelly reduced the Crisis Action Team to a response cell. On 8 January, General Powell sent to all the unified and specified commanders a message complimenting them on their success and their professionalism. As the President had indicated, troops had begun to redeploy by 4 January. Some forty-two hundred had redeployed by 8 January with more to follow until U.S. forces in Panama returned to the pre-JUST CAUSE level below ten thousand troops. On 10 January, Benjamin Colomarco, commander of the Dignity Battalions, surrendered to U.S. forces. On 11 January, General Kelly notified General Thurman that, if he had no objection, the Joint Staff would terminate JUST CAUSE at 1800 that same day. General Thurman agreed. Two hours after termination of JUST CAUSE, General Kelly disbanded the JCS Response Cell.[14]

Chapter 9

Assessments

Some Preliminary Assessments, January–April 1990

In a message to Secretary Cheney, General Lindsay noted that JUST CAUSE demonstrated that both special operations forces and conventional forces had made significant progress toward joint interoperability since the 1983 intervention in Grenada. In Panama, Rangers and the crews of Air Force gunships worked together effectively while exercising great restraint in the use of firepower. The special operations task forces of Army, Navy, and Air Force also coordinated their efforts. General Lindsay also noted the accuracy and timeliness of tactical intelligence; the effective support by civil affairs and psychological operations specialists; and the well-coordinated, responsive actions of logistical units.[1]

In an interview with the *Army Times* on 26 February 1990, General Stiner expressed his satisfaction with the operation:

> JUST CAUSE...validated that what we are doing is right...that the training program...is exactly as it should be.... We expect tough, realistic training of our troops, and this included live-fire and night operations. Our training program paid off in spades in Panama and that's the reason you saw the discipline, the efficiency, the effectiveness and the proficiency that was demonstrated by our troops.... JUST CAUSE was a joint operation in every sense of the word. Cooperation among all services was absolutely outstanding....Each service had unique and important capabilities that were needed to perform this mission.... First of all, we received clear guidance from the national command authority level of what was expected. Secondly, we were allowed to prepare a plan in detail to accomplish that. Third, we briefed that plan all the way up through the decisionmaking authority, and that plan was approved. Fourth, we were allowed sufficient time to conduct detailed rehearsals for its execution. And fifth, when conditions dictated that it should be executed, we were allowed to execute it without changes to the plan. And that was very germane in the outcome of Operation JUST CAUSE.[2]

General Kelly and the Joint Operations Division attributed the success of JUST CAUSE to several factors. During nearly two years of deliberate planning and three months of "fine tuning," the Joint Staff, USCINCSO, and tactical commanders had carefully crafted and coordinated their efforts. Simplicity characterized both the operation order for JUST CAUSE and its chain of command. If there was a planning weakness, it was the lack of detailed attention to post-combat operations and the civil affairs personnel needed to carry them out.[3] General Thurman and General Stiner were outstanding commanders who could be relied on to do their jobs with minimal supervision. General Powell supported both men with staffing and resources. They justified Powell's confidence by the thoroughness with which they rehearsed their forces. These rehearsals precluded many of the mistakes associated with earlier contingency operations.[4]

Operationally, JUST CAUSE did have a major advantage in that nearly half of the operational forces were present in Panama before the trigger event of 16 December. The substantial U.S. presence in Panama facilitated the insertion into Panama before D-Day of special operations forces and the operational chain of command for Joint Task Force South. The U.S. military presence also provided a foundation for speedy force development and the logistical buildup. Without a successful deployment, the forces on the ground could not have executed JUST CAUSE. The deployment depended upon refueling from SAC, aircover from LANTCOM and TAC, and the MAC airlift.[5]

Although General Powell admitted that "there are bound to be one or two glitches in an operation as complex as this," both he and Secretary Cheney were very satisfied with JUST CAUSE. In an interview in Panama in early January 1990, General Powell spoke of the "unfaltering commitment of the troops who successfully carried out the complex missions of JUST CAUSE....In all the combat and training operations I have ever been involved in, I have never seen one as complex as this executed and planned as well." In an interview on 27 March 1990, Secretary Dick Cheney said: "JUST CAUSE showed what we're capable of....I feel very, very good about the overall quality of the operation, the quality of advice we got, and the professionalism with which [the military] carried out the operation."[6]

The Impact of Goldwater-Nichols on JUST CAUSE

The transmission of guidance on Panama contingency planning from the national command authorities to General Thurman and General Stiner reflected changes enacted by the Goldwater-Nichols Defense Reorganization Act of 1986. That act made the Chairman of the Joint Chiefs of Staff—instead of the corporate Joint Chiefs of Staff—the chief military adviser to the President, the Secretary of Defense, the Secretary of State, and the National Security Council. Thus, during the planning for BLUE SPOON, Secretary Cheney worked through General Powell. This practice eliminated the time-consuming deliberation within the Joint Chiefs of Staff that had been needed to win their approval.[7]

The Goldwater-Nichols Act also made the Joint Staff directly responsible to the Chairman instead of to the Joint Chiefs of Staff. It was no longer necessary to delay operational planning decisions to allow for coordination and staffing with the services in preparation for JCS approval. During the planning for BLUE SPOON, General Kelly, and commanders and planners in Fort Bragg and Panama briefed the Chairman frequently, but the Joint Chiefs of Staff rarely. Recognizing the expertise of the Service Chiefs, however, General Powell consulted them on service-related matters affecting the plan.[8]

The Chairman, General Kelly, and Admiral Shaefer briefed the Joint Chiefs on the shooting of Lieutenant Paz and the revised version of BLUE SPOON at General Powell's quarters on 17 December. At that time the JCS agreed to the execution of the plan virtually as written. In General Kelly's view, JCS approval would not have been so readily obtained before the Goldwater-Nichols Act. Under the old system, the Joint Chiefs might have spent more effort on apportioning missions and the forces to be employed. After Goldwater-Nichols became law, neither Admiral Crowe nor General Powell encouraged such activity.

Common sense dictated a predominant role for the Army. Nearly thirteen thousand Army troops were already in Panama, and Panama fell within the area of operations of a unified command dominated by the Army. Planners did use those Marine and naval forces readily at hand for the operation. The Air Force played a larger role than the maritime services because of the Army's dependence upon it for airlift, logistical support, suppression of antiaircraft fire, and interdiction.[9]

Not everyone agreed that the streamlined chain of command used in BLUE SPOON depended upon Goldwater-Nichols. In General Powell's view, the Secretary of Defense had always had the choice of working through the Joint Chiefs of Staff, through the Chairman alone, or of taking personal command of an operation. Ample historical precedent supported his view. During the Vietnam War and the Yom Kippur War of 1973, the Secretary of Defense usually worked solely through the Chairman in transmitting guidance to the commanders. During the U.S. intervention in Grenada in 1983, Secretary Caspar Weinberger had made the Chairman, General John W. Vessey, Jr., U.S. Army, the *de facto* commander for the operation.[10]

Goldwater-Nichols gave additional authority to the commanders of the unified and specified commands. General Thurman exerted strong guidance on the makeup of the chain of command below his headquarters; he had practically insisted that General Stiner be his tactical commander. Thurman then placed both the JTFPM and the JSOTF under Stiner and gave him wide latitude in their employment.[11]

In turn, General Stiner subdivided the JTFPM and the JSOTF into nine separate task forces. He decentralized command below his headquarters to allow separate commanders, dispersed over a wide area, maximum independence and flexibility. After H-Hour, General Stiner envisioned his principal mission as supplying each of the nine task force commanders with all the resources they needed to attain their objectives without awaiting the movements of other units. A chain of command streamlined at the national level and broadened at the tactical level facilitated timely execution and support of JUST CAUSE.[12]

The period 28-29 December marked a turning point in the command relationship between General Powell and his two field commanders. Until 28 December, General Powell had taken pains not to intrude in the combat operations of JUST CAUSE or the early civil affairs operations of PROMOTE LIBERTY. By that time, politico-military factors loomed larger than military ones. From General Powell's point of view, General Thurman and General Stiner were being asked to make decisions of a politically sensitive nature. Three cases proved awkward, if not embarrassing, for Secretary Cheney and the President: the apparent use of rock music to harrass occupants of the *Nunciatura;* the detention of the Cuban ambassador on 28 December; and on 29 December, the illegal search of the Nicaraguan embassy. For that reason, on 28 and 29 December, General Powell played a more active role in the non-tactical aspects of JUST CAUSE by providing explicit and frequent guidance to his two field commanders.[13] These changes reflected Powell's ready access to both the President and Secretary of Defense and to the other agencies of the federal government, particularly the Department of State; and his ability to use their input to provide detailed politico-military guidance to the operational commanders.

NOTES

While the text of this study has been declassified, some of its sources remain classified. Sources noted as in possession of Secretariat Joint Staff/Historical Division (SJS/HisDiv) are now in the Joint History Office, Office of the Chairman of the Joint Chiefs of Staff (OCJCS).

Chapter 1
Background of the Crisis

[1] App, JCSM 75-87 to SecDef, 9 Jun 87, JCS 1976/686, TS, JMF 922/520 (13 May 87).

[1] J-3 Briefing, Opn JUST CAUSE, 2 Apr 90, U, J-3/Joint Operations Div (JOD)/Western Hemisphere Branch (WHEM). USSOUTHCOM Hist Rpt. 1988, S, pp. 20–21, 128, 133–134, and 153.

[1] National Military Intelligence Support Team (NMIST), Panama Intelligence Task Force (ITF) to USSOUTHCOM J-2, 280150Z Dec 89, S, Pan. Binder, J-5/Dep Dir Pol Mil Aff (DDPMA)/WHEM. Msg, USCINCSO to JCS, 140325Z Apr 88, TS, Pan. Fact Bk, J-3/JOD/WHEM.

[1] Msg, USCINCSO to JCS, 140325 Apr 88, TS, Pan. Fact Bk, J-3/JOD/WHEM.

[1] Interv, Dr. Ronald H. Cole, Historical Division, with LTG Thomas H. Kelly, USA, Dir J-3, 22 May 90, Secretariat Joint Staff/Historical Division (SJS/HisDiv). Transcript, Testimony of LTG Kelly, J-3, and RADM Edward D. Sheafer, USN, Deputy Director for JCS Support (DIA), before Senate Armed Services Committee (SASC), 22 Dec 89, TS, Office of the Chairman JCS (OCJCS)/Legal and Legislative Council (LLC). Interv Cole w/LTC (P) James Shane, USA, J-3/ JOD/WHEM, 2 Apr 90, S, SJS/HisDiv. Msg, JCS to USCINCSO, 281944Z Apr 89, TS, Pan. Fact Bk, J-3/JOD/WHEM.

[1] Msgs, USCICS to JCS, 140325Z, 140326Z, 140327Z, and 150125Z Apr 88, TS, Pan. Fact Bk, J-3/JOD/WHEM. Kelly Interview. Memo, COL James F. Hennessee, USA, XO, USSOUTHCOM, to Dr. Ronald H. Cole, Historian, Joint Staff, 14 May 90, S, SJS/HisDiv. Note: The Hennessee memo answered follow-up questions to the interview of GEN Thurman conducted by Dr. Cole on 8 Mar 90.

[1] Msg, USCINCSO to JCS 140325Z Apr 88, TS, Pan. Fact Bk, J-3/JOD/WHEM. Kelly Interview. Shane Interview.

[1] Msg, USCINCSO to JCS 140327Z Apr 88, TS, Pan. Fact Bk, J-3/JOD/WHEM. Kelly Interview. Shane Interview.

[1] Kelly Interview.

[1] Hennessee Memo. Interv, Cole w/LTC Timothy L. McMahon, USA, Chief of Plans, G-3, XVIIIth Airborne Corps, 26 Apr 90, U, SJS/HisDiv. Press Conference, *Army Times* et al. w/LTG Carl Stiner, USA, CG, XVIIIth Airborne Corps, 26 Feb 90, U, SJS/HisDiv. Dr. Theresa Kraus, USA Center of Military History, Working Chronology, Operation JUST CAUSE, June 1988. Woerner Interview.

[1] Msg, USCINCSO to JCS, 272115Z Oct 88, TS, Tab D, TP for J-3 for Mtg with J-3s, USSOUTHCOM and FORSCOM on 8 Nov 88, 7 Nov 88, TS, J-3/JOD/WHEM. Hennessee Memo.

[1] TP for J-3 Mtg w/USSOUTHCOM and FORSCOM, 8 Nov 88, 7 Nov 88, TS, J-3/JOD/WHEM. Kelly Interview.

[1] Kraus Chronology.

[1] Ibid. Kelly Interview. Interv, Cole w/Dr. Lawrence A. Yates, Hist., CSI, USA C&GS College, Fort Leavenworth, KS, at the Pentagon, 15 Nov 1990, U.

[1] Interv, Ronald H. Cole and Willard J. Webb, Historical Division, with Secretary Richard B. Cheney, 27 Mar 90, S, SJS/HisDiv.

[1] Interv, Ronald H. Cole, Historical Division, with BG David C. Meade, USA, J-5/DDPMA, 21 May 90, S, SJS/HisDiv.

[1] NSD 17, 22 Jul 89, S, Chairman's Study Group (CSG—Col Jerrold P. Allen, USAF), OCJCS.

[1] Ibid.

[1] Woerner Interview. A report in the *Washington Post*, 22 Jul 89, p. A20, alleged that President Bush had removed General Woerner for two reasons. The previous February, Woerner had criticized Bush for not dealing adequately with the crisis in Panama. After the overturning of Panamanian elections in May 1989, moreover, conservative senators who had visited Woerner complained to President Bush that Woerner was "not tough enough in dealing with Noriega's provocations against U.S. troops." In the interview with Dr. Cole, General Woerner speculated that the senators' criticisms may have influenced President Bush to remove him.

[1] *Washington Post*, 22 Jul 89, p. A20. Cheney Interview. Kelly Interview.

[1] Kelly and Cheney Interviews.

[1] Hennessee Memo.

[1] Interv, Ronald H. Cole w/GEN Maxwell R. Thurman, USA, USCINCSO, 8 Mar 90, S, SJS/HisDiv. Kelly Transcript.

[1] Thurman Interview. Hennessee Memo. Kelly Transcript.

[1] Interv, Ronald H. Cole and Willard J. Webb, Historical Division, with GEN Colin L. Powell, USA, Chairman of the Joint Chiefs of Staff, 13 Feb 90, S, SJS/HisDiv.

[1] The account of the coup attempt was taken from the following sources: Transcript Testimony, SecDef, GEN Powell, and LTG Kelly, SASC and Senate Select Committee on Intelligence (SSCI), 6 Oct 89, TS; SASC & SSCI Joint Hearing on Panama w/GEN Thurman, 17 Oct 89, S; Trans., Test., GEN Thurman, HASC, 20 Nov 89, TS; OCJCS/LLC. Powell, Cheney and Thurman Interviews.

[1] Ibid. Powell Testimony.

[1] Ibid.

[1] Ibid. Powell Interview.

Chapter 2
After the Coup Attempt: Accelerated Joint Planning and Preparation, 3 October–15 December 1989

[1] Thurman Interview. Hennessee Memo. Powell Interview.

[1] Thurman Interview.

[1] Ibid. Powell Interview. Cheney Interview. Powell later said, "Many people thought we were 'trolling' for an opportunity to invade. We were not. We just wanted to be prepared to go immediately when the President made the decision to do so."

[1] Thurman Interview. Hennessee Memo. Powell Interview. Cheney Interview.

[1] Ibid.

[1] Powell Interview.

[1] Msg, CINCFOR to CDR, U.S.CATA, Ft Leavenworth, KS, DA, WASH, 261340Z Feb 90, S, SJS/HisDiv.

[1] OPERATION ORDERS Panama Folder, TS, J-3/JOD/WHEM. File contains OPORD 1-90 which is reference for following paragraphs discussing its details.

[1] Kelly Interview. Hennessee Memo. Powell Interview.

[1] Cheney Interview.

[1] JTFSO OPLAN 90-2, HQ, XVIIIth Airborne Corps, 3 Nov 89, TX, J-3/JOD/WHEM.

[1] J-3 Briefing, LTC Shane, 2 Apr 90, S, J-3/JOD/WHEM.

[1] JTFSO OPLAN 90-2, HQ, XVIIIth Airborne Corps, 3 Nov 89, TS, J-3/JOD/WHEM.

[1] Stiner Conference. Kraus Chronology.

[1] *USTRANSCOM Hist, 1989*, S, pp. 62–63.

[1] Thurman Interview. Hennessee Memo.

[1] Thurman Interview. Msg, USCINCSO to CDR, XVIIIth Abn Corps et al., 091858 Nov 89, TS, Pro Rata Msgs, Bk 3, J-3/JOD/WHEM. Kelly Transcript.

[1] Msg, USSOUTHCOM to CJCS 200030Z Nov 89, S, CJCS Files. Thurman Interview.
[1] Thurman Interview. Msg, CINCFOR to CDR, USCATA, Ft Leavenworth, KS, and DA, WASH, 261340Z Feb 90, S. SJS/HisDiv. Stiner Conference.
[1] Cheney Interview.

Chapter 3
Trigger Events, The Decision to Intervene and Final Preparations for H-Hour, 15–19 December 1989

[1] Thurman Interview. *NY Times*, 21 Dec 89, p. A18.
[1] J-3 Chron Sum, 16 Dec 89, S, J-3/JOD/WHEM. Thurman Interview. National Military Support Team (NMIST) Debriefing , J-3 Chron Sum, 17 Dec 89, S, J-3/JOD/WHEM.
[1] Powell Interview. Cheney Interview. Thurman Interview. J-3 Chron Sum, 16 Dec 89, S.
[1] Thurman Interview.
[1] Cheney Interview.
[1] Powell Interview.
[1] This and the following three paragraphs derive from: Cheney Interview. Powell Interview. Shane Interview. Kelly Transcript. Quotes taken from Powell Interview.
[1] Kelly Interview.
[1] Ibid.
[1] Kelly Interview. Thurman Interview. J-3 Chron Sum, 18 Dec 89, TS, J-3/JOD/WHEM. Msg, CINCFOR to CDR, U.S.CATA, Ft Leavenworth, KS, and DA, WASH, 261340Z Feb 90, S, SJS/HisDiv. Kraus Chronology.
[1] Powell Inteview. Cheney Interview.
[1] Ibid.
[1] Ibid. This paragraph and the next two are also based on the following: Thurman Interview. Stiner Conference. Kelly Transcript. Powell Interview, 10 Dec 90, S, J-3 Chron Sum, 18 Dec 89, S, J-3/JOD/WHEM.
[1] Msg, CJCS to USCINCSO et al., 182325Z Dec 89, TS (Pro Rata), JCS Specat Traffic Log, J-3/ JOD/WHEM. Msg, CINCFOR to CDR, XVIIIth Abn Ccrps, 190100Z Dec 89, JUST CAUSE Specat Traffic Log, J-3/JOD/WHEM.
[1] Kelly Interview.
[1] Powell Interview.
[1] Sources used for the airlift include: Kelly Interview. Msg, CINCFOR to CDR, USCATA, Ft Leavenworth, KS, and DA, WASH, 261340Z Feb 90, S. SJS/HisDiv. J-3 Chron Sum, TS, J-3/ JOD/WHEM. Kraus Chronology.
[1] Kraus Chronology.
[1] Msg, USCINCLANT to CINCLANTFLT, 190543Z Dec 89, TS; Msg, CINCAFLANT to CINCLANT, 200023Z Dec 89, TS; Msg, HQ, AFLAT to CINCSAC, 200352Z Dec 89, TS; Specat Traffic Log, J-3/JOD/WHEM. USCINCSO JUST CAUSE Sitrep 001, 210947Z Dec 89, S, PM Sitreps, J-3/JOD/WHEM. *History of SAC, 1989*, 19 Sep 90, S, pp. 31–32.
[1] Sources for evidence of a compromise derive from: Kelly Interview. Stiner Conference. J-3 Chron Sum, 19 Dec 89, TS, J-3/JOD/WHEM. Kraus Chronology. Msg, CINCFOR to CDR, USACATA, Fort Leavenworth, KS, and DA, WASH, 261340Z Feb 90, S, SJS/HisDiv. Patrick E. Tyler, "Pentagon Corrects 'Panama Invasion Leaks' Report," *Washington Post*, 13 Mar 90, p. A23.
[1] Powell Interview. Kelly Interview.
[1] Stiner Conference. Note: The bombing by the two F-117As on D-Day better explains the alertness of the PDF troops at Rio Hato. (See p. 47)
[1] Powell Interview. Kelly Interview. Tyler, "Pentagon Corrects . . . Leaks' Report," *Washington Post*, 13 Mar 90, p. A23.
[1] Msg, COMJSOTF, Howard Air Force Base to COMJTFSO, Ft Clayton, PN, 200214Z Dec 89, TS, JUST CAUSE Specat Traffic Log, J-3/JOD/WHEM.

[1] Cheney Interview. Thurman Interview.

Chapter 4
D-day, Wednesday, 20 December 1989

[1] International Institute for Strategic Studies, "Panama," *The Military Balance, 1989–1990*, (London, 1989), pp. 198–199.

[1] J-3 Briefing, Opn JUST CAUSE, 2 Apr 90, U, J-3/JOD/WHEM.

[1] J-3 Briefing, Opn JUST CAUSE, 2 Apr 90, U; USCINCSO, JUST CAUSE Sitrep 001, 210947Z Dec 89, S, PM Sitreps; J-3 TP, "JUST CAUSE Recap for CJCS Visit to Paris," 8 Jan 90, S, J-3 Cell SOA Info Binder 5; J-3/JOD/WHEM.

[1] J-3 TP, "JUST CAUSE Recap for CJCS Visit to Paris," 8 Jan 90, S, J-3 Cell Special Operations Activity (SOA) Info Binder 5, JTFSO Organization Slides, Tab R, TS, J-3 Cell SOA Info Binder 3; J-3/JOD/WHEM.

[1] J-3 Briefing, Opn JUST CAUSE, 2 Apr 90, S; J-3 Chron Sum, 20 Dec 89, TS; J-3/JOD/WHEM. Kraus Chronology.

[1] J-3 Chron Sum, 20 Dec 89, TS, J-3/JOD/WHEM. Kraus Chronology.

[1] Ibid. Interv, Cole w/Gen Powell, LTG Kelly, and MAJ Melnyk, 20 Dec 90, S, SJS/HisDiv. *Washington Times*, 12 Apr 90, p. A4. *NY Times*, 11 Apr 90, p. 19. Scott Shuger, "'New Weapons, Old Problems,'"*The Washington Monthly* (Oct 1990); pp. 43–49.

[1] J-3 Briefing, Opn JUST CAUSE, S, J-3/JOD/WHEM. Stiner Conference. *NY Times*, 21 Dec 89, p. A1.

[1] J-3 Chron Sum, TS, J-3/JOD/WHEM. Stiner Conference. Kraus Chronology. USCINCSO JUST CAUSE Sitrep 001, 210947Z Dec 89, S, Pan. Sitreps, J-3/JOD/WHEM.

[1] USCINCSO JUST CAUSE Sitrep 001, 210947Z Dec 89, Panama Sitreps; USSOUTHCOM Intel Sum, 0637, 20 Dec 89, J-3 Chron Sum, TS; J-3/JOD/WHEM.

[1] J-3 Chron Sum, TS. USCINCSO JUST CAUSE Sitrep 001, 210947Z Dec 89, S, Panama Sitreps, J-3/JOD/WHEM.

[1] USCINCSO JUST CAUSE Sitrep 001, 210947Z Dec 89, S, Panama Sitreps; U.S.SOUTHCOM Intel Sum, 0637, 20 Dec 89, S; J-3 Chron Sum, TS; J-3/JOD/WHEM. Stiner Conference. *Washington Post*, 21 Dec 89, p. A37.

[1] Ibid.

[1] Ibid. J-3 TP, "JUST CAUSE Recap for CJCS Visit to Paris," 8 Jan 90, S, J-3 Cell SOA Info Binder 5, J-3/JOD/WHEM.

[1] Ibid.

[1] J-3 Chron Sum, esp. USSOUTHCOM Intel Sum 0637, 20 Dec 89, TS; USCINCSO JUST CAUSE Sitrep 001, 210947Z Dec 89, S, Panama Sitreps; J-3/JOD/WHEM. Kraus Chronology. Stiner Conference.

[1] See sources in footnote above.

[1] Stiner Conference. USCINCSO JUST CAUSE Sitrep 001, 210947Z Dec 89, S, Panama Sitreps, J-3/JOD/WHEM. J-3 TP, "JUST CAUSE Recap for 8 Jan 90, S, J-3 Cell SOA Info Binder 5. CJCS Visit to Paris."

[1] Ibid.

[1] Meade Interview.

[1] Presidential Address, 20 Dec 89, *Weekly Compilation of Presidential Documents*, vol. 25, pp. 1974–1975.

[1] *NY Times*, 21 Dec 90, p. A19.

[1] Memo, SecDef to SecsMilDeps, CJCS, UnderSecsDef, et al., "Modification of DOD Directive 5525.5, "DOD Cooperation with Civilian Law Enforcement Officials (U)," 20 Dec 89, U, SJS/HisDiv.

[1] Ibid.

[1] MFR, SecDef Dick Cheney, "Approval Consistent with Revised DOD Directive 5525.5, 'DOD Cooperation with Civilian Law Enforcement Officials,' of Assistance to Law Enforcement Apprehension of Manuel Noriega of Panama," 20 Dec 89, U, SJS/HisDiv.

Chapter 5
Issues in the National Military Command Center: Civil Affairs Reservists, the Media Pool, and U.S. Hostages

[1] Cheney Interview. Thurman Interview.
[1] Msg, JCS to USCINCSO, 200006Z Dec 89, JUST CAUSE Specat Traffic Catalog; Memo, Dir J-3 to Service Chiefs, 200300Z Dec 89, TS, JOD Response Cell, Bk l; J-3/JOD/WHEM.
[1] Ibid. Kelly Interview.
[1] Kelly Interview. Meade Interview. Cheney Interview.
[1] Meade Interview.
[1] Msg, Joint Staff to White House et al., 201927Z Dec 89, S, JUST CAUSE Specat Traffic Log, J-3/JOD/WHEM.
[1] Msg, USCINCSO to CJCS, 200819Z Dec 89, TS; Memo, DJS to CJCS, 20 Dec 89, S; J-3 Cell SOA Info Binder l.
[1] Msg, USCINCSO to JCS, 202055Z Dec 89, TS, J-3 Cell SOA Info Binder l.
[1] Kelly Interview. Cheney Interview.
[1] Cheney Interview.
[1] Powell Interview.
[1] Msgs, SecDef to USCINCSO, 200428Z Dec 89 and 200637Z Dec 89, S, JUST CAUSE Specat Traffic Log, J-3/JOD/WHEM.
[1] USCINCSO JUST CAUSE Sitrep 001, 210947Z Dec 89, and Sitrep 002, 221230Z Dec 89, S; Panama Sitreps, J-3/JOD/WHEM. Msg, OASD/PA to CINCFOR et al., 201957Z Dec 89, U, J-3 Cell SOA Info Binder 4.
[1] Ibid. Kelly Interview.
[1] Cheney Interview. Powell Interview. Kelly Interview.
[1] Memo for Correspondents by Fred Hoffman, "Review of Panama Pool Deployment, December 1989," 20 Mar 90, U, SJS/HisDiv.
[1] J-3 Chron Sum, 20 Dec 89, TS, J-3/JOD/WHEM. Kraus Chronology.
[1] Ibid.
[1] Cheney Interview. Powell Interview. Kelly Interview.
[1] J-3 Chron Sum, 20 Dec 89, TS, J-3/JOD/WHEM. Kraus Chronology.

Chapter 6
Last Combat, Civil Affairs, and the Hunt for Noriega 21–24 December 1989

[1] Msg, CINCFOR to CDR, USACATA, and DA, 261340Z Feb 90, S, SJS/HisDiv.
[1] J-3 Briefing, Operation JUST CAUSE, 2 Apr 90, S; J-3 Chron Sum, 21 Dec 89, TS; J-3/ JOD/WHEM.
[1] Ibid. USCINCSO JUST CAUSE Sitrep 003, 231150Z Dec 89, S; J-3 Chron Sum, 21 Dec 89, TS; J-3/JOD/WHEM.
[1] Ibid. Msg, CJCS to CINCFOR et al., 222116Z Dec 89, S, J-3 Cell SOA Info Binder l.
[1] USCINCSO JUST CAUSE Sitrep 004, 241000Z Dec 89, S, J-3/JOD/WHEM.
[1] J-3 Chron Sum, TS, J-3/JOD/WHEM.
[1] Ibid.
[1] Msg, CJCS to USCINCSO et al., 211453Z Dec 89, S; Msg, CJCS to CSA, 211457Z Dec 89, S; J-3 Cell SOA Binder 1, J-3/JOD/WHEM. CJCS Sitrep 007, 262028Z Dec 89, S, J-3 Cell SOA Info Binder 2, J-3/JOD/WHEM. Kelly Interview.
[1] Ibid. Msg, CJCS to USCINCSO et al., 211415Z Dec 89, JOD Response Cell, Book 1.
[1] J-3 Chron Sum, 22 Dec 89, TS, J-3/JOD/WHEM.
[1] Memo, Bernard Aronson, STATE, to BG Meade, DepDirPolMil/J-5, 1400, 23 Dec 89, S, J-5/DDPMA Panama Binder, J-5/WHEM.
[1] Msg, CJCS to USCINCSO, 231924Z Dec 89, S, JOD Response Cell, Bk 1, J-3/JOD/WHEM.

[1] Msg, USCINCSO to CJCS, 241535Z Dec 89, TS, J-3 Cell SOA Info Binder 2, J-3/ JOD/WHEM. Thurman Interview. Kraus Chronology.

[1] J-3 Chron Sum, 24 Dec 89, S, J-3/JOD/WHEM.

[1] Kelly Interview. Meade Interview. Memo, MG Richard Loeffke, Chmn, IADB, to DJS, "Meeting w/Secy Gen OAS, 21 Dec 89 (U)," S, J-5/DDPMA Panama Binder, J-5/WHEM.

[1] J-3 Chron Sum, 21, 22, & 23 Dec 89, S, J-3/JOD/WHEM.

[1] Ibid. Transcript, Testimony, RADM Sheafer, J-2 Rep (DIA), SASC, 22 Dec 89, TS, OCJCS/LLC.

[1] USCINCSO JUST CAUSE Sitrep 003, 231150Z Dec 89, S, J-3/JOD/WHEM. J-3 Chron Sum, 23 Dec 89, S, J-3/JOD/WHEM.

[1] Msg, USCINCSO to CJCS, 241535Z Dec 89, TS, J-3 Cell SOA Info Binder 2, J-3/JOD/ WHEM.

[1] J-3 Chron Sum, 21 Dec 89, S, J-3/JOD/WHEM. Stiner Conference. USCINCSO JUST CAUSE Sitrep 005, 251000Z Dec 89, S, J-3/JOD/WHEM. Powell Interview. Cheney Interview. Meade Interview. MFR, BG Meade, 25 Dec 89, S, J-5/DDPMA, Panama Binder, J-5/WHEM. OPS/INTELL Brief., 1700 EST, 28 Dec 89, S, J-3 Cell SOA Info Binder 3, J-3/JOD/WHEM.

[1] J-3 Chron Sum, 21 Dec 89, S, J-3/JOD/WHEM. Stiner Conference. USCINCSO JUST CAUSE Sitrep 005, 251000Z Dec 89, S, J-3/JOD/WHEM. Powell Interview. Cheney Interview. Meade Interview. MFR, BG Meade, 25 Dec 89, S, J-5/DDPMA, Panama Binder, J-5/WHEM. OPS/INTELL Brief., 1700 EST, 28 Dec 89, S, J-3 Cell SOA Info Binder 3, J-3/JOD/WHEM.

Chapter 7
The *Nunciatura,* 24 December 1989 - 3 January 1990

[1] Powell Interview. Cheney Interview. Msg, Amembassy Rome 00536 to SecState, 101727Z Jan 90, C, J-5/DDPMA (Panama), J-5/WHEM.

[1] Meade Interview.

[1] Powell Interview. Kelly Interview.

[1] Ibid.

[1] J-3, Chron Sum, 24 Dec 89, S, J-3/JOD/WHEM.

[1] "NCA Guidance for Selected Diplomatic Facilities," 25 December 89, C, Tab 18, J-3 Cell SOA Info Binder 3, J-3/JOD/WHEM. J-3 Chron Sum, 25 and 26 Dec 89, TS, J-3/JOD/WHEM.

[1] J-3 Chron Sum, 26 Dec 89, S. Ltr, papal nuncio, Panama, to USCINCSO, Tab I, J-3 Cell SOA Info Binder 2, J-3/JOD/WHEM.

[1] J-3 Chron Sum, 27, 30, and 31 Dec 89, TS. Memo, Actg SecDef to CJCS, 27 Dec 89. TS, J-3 Cell SOA Info Binder 2, J-3/JOD/WHEM.

[1] Thurman Interview. Powell Interview.

[1] J-3 Chron Sum, 28 Dec 89, S, J-3/JOD/WHEM.

[1] Ibid.

[1] Powell Interview. Msg, CJCS to USCINCSO, 292327Z Dec 89, C, J-3 Cell SOA Info Binder 3, J-3/JOD/WHEM.

[1] Memo, LTG Stiner to Joint Staff, 29 Dec 89, S; Msg, State 045454Z to NMCC/CAT, 29 Dec 89, S; J-3 Cell SOA Info Binder 3, J-3/JOD/WHEM.

[1] Ibid.

[1] For this and the following paragraphs see: J-3 Chron Sum, 29 Dec 89, S; CJCS Sitrep 011; 301841Z Dec 89; J-3 Cell SOA Info Binder 3, J-3/JOD/WHEM. Powell Interview. Meade Interview.

[1] Ibid. Msg, Amemb Managua to SecState 07575, "Nicaraguan Government Claim U.S. Forces Break into their Ambassador's Residence in Panama (U)," 300214Z Dec 89, C, J-3 Cell SOA Info Binder 3, J-3/JOD/WHEM.

[1] J-3 Chron Sum, 30 Dec 89, S, J-3/JOD/WHEM. Msg, State 412988 to USCINCSO, "Diplomatic Privileges and Immunities (U)," 310422Z Dec 89, C, J-5/DDPMA/WHEM.

[1] Msg, State 412988 to USCINCSO, "Diplomatic Privileges and Immunities (U)," 310422Z Dec 89, C, J-5/DDPMA/WHEM.

[1] Msg, Amemb Rome 00536 to SecState 101727Z Jan 90, C, J-5/DDPMA/WHEM. Msg, CIA to DIA, "Release of Noriega to Panama Authorities on 30 December," S, 300019Z Dec 89, S, J-3 Cell SOA Info Binder 3, J-3/JOD/WHEM. Msg, USCINCSO to Joint Staff, 260815Z Dec 89, SJS 1778/396-00, TS, JMF 933. Msg, Amemb Rome 00536 to SecState 101727 Jan 90, C; Memo, MG Loeffke to DJS, 27 Dec 89, S; J-5/DDPMA/WHEM. CJCS Sitrep 009 281823Z Dec 89, S, J-3 Cell SOA Info Binder 3, J-3/JOD/WHEM.

[1] J-3 Chron Sum, 29 Dec 90, S, J-3/JOD/WHEM. Ltr, Episcopal Conference of Panama to John Paul II, 29 Dec 89, U, J-3 Cell SOA Binder 3, J-3/JOD/WHEM. Ltr, Pres. Endara to Pope John Paul II, 28 Dec 89, U, J-3/JOD/WHEM.

[1] J-3 Chron Sum, 29 Dec 90, S, J-3/JOD/WHEM. Ltr, Episcopal Conference of Panama to John Paul II, 29 Dec 89, U, J-3 Cell SOA Binder 3, J-3/JOD/WHEM.

[1] Msg, Amemb Panama 00007 to SecState, 011818 Jan 90, U; Msg, Amemb Rome 00536 to SecState 101727 Jan 90, C; J-5/DDPMA/WHEM. CJCS Sitrep 012, 311747Z Dec 89, S, J-3 Cell SOA Info Binder 3, J-3/JOD/WHEM. J-3 Chron Sum, 30 Dec 89, S, J-3/JOD/WHEM.

[1] J-3 Chron Sum, 1 Jan 90, S, J-3/JOD/WHEM. Msg, Amemb Panama to SecState, Info JCS, 082251Z Jan 90, C, Spec, J-5/DDPMA/WHEM. J-3 Chron Sum, 2 Jan 90, S, J-3/JOD/WHEM. J-3 Chron Sum, 2 Jan 90, S, J-3/JOD/WHEM. Msg, Amemb Panama to SecState 082251Z Jan 90, C-Spec, J-5/DDPMA/WHEM.

[1] The above and the ensuing paragraphs derive from the following: J-3 Chron Sum, 3 Jan 90, S; USCINCSO JUST CAUSE 015, 041000Z Jan 90, S; J-3/JOD/WHEM. Msg, Amemb Panama to SecState (info JCS), 082251Z Jan 90, C-Spec, J-5/DDPMA/WHEM.

Chapter 8
The End of Organized Resistance, the Shift to Nationbuilding and Redeployment, 25 December 1989–3 January 1990

[1] USCINCSO JUST CAUSE Sitrep 006, 261050Z Dec 89,S, J-3/JOD/WHEM. CJCS Sitrep 007, 262028Z Dec 89, J-3 Cell SOA Info Binder 2, J-3/JOD/WHEM.

[1] CJCS Sitrep 007, 262028Z Dec 89, S, J-3 Cell SOA Info Binder 2; CJCS Sitrep 009, 281823Z Dec 89, S, J-3 Cell SOA Info Binder 3; J-3/JOD/WHEM. J-3 TP, "JUST CAUSE Recap for CJCS Visit to Paris (U)," 8 Jan 90, S, J-3 Cell SOA Info Binder 5, J-3/JOD/WHEM.

[1] *LA Times*, 24 Apr 90, p. 1. Memo, USCINCSO to JCS, 100105Z Jan 90, C.

[1] Kelly Interview.

[1] CJCS Sitrep 007, 262028Z Dec 89, S; Msg, USCINCSO to Joint Staff, 260845Z Dec 89, S; CJCS Sitrep 008, 272213Z, S; J-3 Cell SOA Info Binder 2, J-3/JOD/WHEM. J-3 TP, "JUST CAUSE Recap for CJCS Visit to Paris (U)," 8 Jan 90, S, J-3 Cell Info Binder 5, J-3/JOD-WHEM.

[1] Msg, USCINCSO to CJCS, 262235Z Dec 89, C, J-3 Cell SOA Info Binder 2, J-3/JOD/WHEM.

[1] Msg, USCINCSO to CJCS, 281808Z Dec 89, S, SJS 1778/399-00, S, File 933 (CY 1989).

[1] Memo, CINCSOUTH to CJCS, 1 Jan 90, S, J-3 Cell SOA Info Binder 4, J-3/JOD/WHEM.

[1] J-3 Chron Sum, 2 Jan 90, S, J-3/JOD/WHEM.

[1] Msg, Amemb Panama 00028 to SecState, 022202Z Jan 90, S-Spec, J-5/DDPMA (Panama), J-5/WHEM.

[1] Ibid.

[1] USCINCSO JUST CAUSE/PROMOTE LIBERTY Sitrep 015, 041000Z Jan 90, S, J-3/JOD/ WHEM. Msg, CJCS to USCINCSO et al., 032235Z Jan 90 and Msg, CJCS to USCINCSO, 032236Z Jan 90, S; J-3 Cell SOA Info Binder 4, J-3/JOD/WHEM.

[1] Presidential Statement, 3 Jan 90, *Weekly Compilation of Presidential Documents*, vol. 26, pp. 8–9.

[1] J-3 Chron Sum, 8 and 11 Jan 90, S, J-3/JOD/WHEM. Msg, Joint Staff to USCINCSO, 061621Z Jan 90, S, J-3 Cell SOA Info Binder 4; J-3 TP, "JUST CAUSE Recap for CJCS Visit to

Paris," 8 Jan 90, S, J-3 Cell SOA Info Binder 5; Memo, Joint Staff to CSA et al. , 11 Jan 90, U, J-3 Cell SOA Info Binder 5; J-3/JOD/WHEM. Msg, COMJTFSO Sitrep 025 to USCINCSO, 110445Z Jan 90, S, J-5/DDPMA/WHEM

Chapter 9
Assessments

[1] Msg, USCINCSOC to SecDef et al., 241720Z Jan 90, U, SJS/HisDiv.

[1] Stiner Conference.

[1] J-3 Briefing, Opn JUST CAUSE, ca. 2 Apr 90, S, J-3/JOD/WHEM. Kelly Interview.

[1] J-3 Briefing, Opn JUST CAUSE, ca. 2 Apr 90, S, J-3/JOD/WHEM.

[1] Ibid.

[1] Air Force News Service, Internal Information Service, News Center, Kelly Air Force Base, TX, 10-16 Jan 90, U, p. 3. Cheney Interview.

[1] Goldwater-Nichols DOD Reorganization Act of 1986, PL 99-433, 1 Oct 86, secs. 151, 153. Kelly Interview. Cheney Interview. Kelly Transcript. J-3 Briefing, Opn JUST CAUSE, 2 Apr 90, J-3/
JOD/WHEM.

[1] Ibid. Powell Interview.

[1] Kelly Transcript. Kelly Interview. See discussion of friendly forces, pp. 45–46.

[1] Powell Interview. Interv, Cole w/GEN Vessey, 25 Mar 87, S; SJS/HisDiv.

[1] Kelly Interview. Thurman Interview. Shane Interview. Kelly Transcript. J-3 Briefing, Opn JUST CAUSE, 2 Apr 90, U, J-3/JOD/WHEM.

[1] Ibid. Stiner Conference.

[1] Powell Interview.

INDEX

Abrams, Elliot: 6
Airborne Warning and Control System (AWACS): 20, 33, 35
Aircraft
  AC-130: 23, 35, 63
  AH-64: 63
  C-5: 33
  C-130: 33–34, 63
  C-141: 33–34, 52
  E-3 (See AWACS)
  EC-130: 23
  EF-111: 23
  F-15: 33
  F-16: 33, 35
  F-117: 23
  F-117A: 30–33, 38–39, 41
  KC-10: 33
  KC-135: 33
  UH-60: 35
Air Force forces (AFFOR): 68
Albrook Air Force Station, C.Z.: 7, 38
Andrews Air Force Base, Md: 47
Armijo, Roberto: 51, 53–54
Aronson, Bernard: 11, 42
ATLANTIC, Task Force (7th Infantry Division (L) and 82d Airborne Division): 21–22, 38–40, 51
Atwood, Donald: 21, 59

Baker, James: 11, 17, 29, 43, 57, 62–63, 67
BANNER SAVIOR, Operation: 14, 17
BAYONET, Task Force (193d Infantry Brigade): 2, 21–22, 38, 40, 55
Beirut: 1, 25
Berlocco, Monsignor Giacinto: 62–63
BLACK, Task Force (SOUTHCOM Special Forces): 20, 38
BLIND LOGIC, Operation: 8–9, 21, 46–47. *See* PROMOTE LIBERTY, Operation.
BLUE, Task Force (Army Special Mission and Navy Special Warfare Units): 20, 38
BLUE SPOON, Operation: 11, 13–14, 16, 19, 29. *See* JUST CAUSE

Operation.
Bridge of the Americas: 20–21, 23, 37–38, 40
Brown, Richard: 12, 42
Bush, George H. W.: 1–3, 11–12, 14, 16, 25, 29, 30, 32–33, 35, 42, 47, 53, 58, 60, 68
Bushnell, John: 35, 53, 58
Butler, Lt Gen George L.: 12

C-141 (Starlifter) icing problem: 33
Cabrera, Alberto: 60
Calderón, Ricardo Arias: 10, 33, 35–36, 43, 58, 68
Carcel Modelo prison: 22, 38
Carlucci, Frank C.: 7, 11
Carns, Lt Gen Michael P. C.: 46
Carter, Jimmy: 10, 29
Castillo, Capt Ivan: 56
Castrejon, Colonel Arnulfo: 56
casualties: 38–41, 52, 65–66
CBS News: 34
Chairman of the Joint Chiefs of Staff (CJCS): 1, 46, 75
Charleston Air Force Base, S.C.: 31, 33
Cheney, Richard B.: 1, 11, 13,15–18, 21, 25, 27–32, 35, 43–49, 51, 56–57, 59, 71–74
Cisneros, General Marc: 7, 9, 15, 24–25, 55, 57, 59–60, 63, 67
Civil affairs. *See* BLIND LOGIC, Operation; PROMOTE LIBERTY, Operation
Civil-military operations task force (CMOTF): 52–53
Coco Solo Naval Air Station, Pan.: 22, 40
Colomarco, Benjamin: 52, 69
Colón: 8, 20–22, 25, 37, 39, 42, 49, 53
Comandancia: 2, 7–8, 14–16, 20–22, 27–29, 34, 37–41, 47
Commander in Chief (CINC): 1–3, 10, 24
Conventional force operations: 13

Operation
Owens, RADM William A.: 27

PACIFIC, Task Force (82d Airborne
Division): 21, 22, 39, 49
PACOM (See U.S. Pacific Command)
Palastra, GEN Joseph T., Jr.: 10
Palma, Manuel Solis: 6
Panama
  elections: 2, 10; geography
  and demography, 5; military,
  see Panama Defense Forces
Panama Canal: 5, 7
Panama Canal Commission (PCC)housing
  areas: 18
Panama Canal Treaty: 5 , 12
Panama Defense Forces (PDF): 2,
  6–8, 37; abolishment, 29, 51;
  resistance, 31, 40–43
Panamanian military units
  1st Infantry Company: 22, 37
  2d Infantry Company: 37
  3d Infantry Company: 65
  5th Rifle Company: 22, 37, 40, 51
  6th Rifle Company: 22, 37, 40
  7th Rifle Company: 22, 37, 40, 51
  8th Rifle Company: 22, 37, 39,
  12th Cavalry Squadron: 37, 41
  Battalion 2000: 22, 34, 37, 41
Panama Viejo: 20–22, 38, 47, 54
Papal *Nunciatura*
  Noriega asylum: 3, 10, 55–60,
  62–63
Paz, 1st LT Robert: 2, 27–28, 73
Paitilla Airfield: 20, 22, 38, 47,
  54
Papal nuncio (See Laboa): 56–57,
  59, 68
Pecora River Bridge: 41
PLANAMONTANA contingency plan: 55
Poindexter, VADM John M.: 6
Policy Coordinating Committee (PCC):
  11, 42
Pope Air Force Base, N.C.: 31, 33
Posse Comitatus Act (18 U.S.C.
  1385): 43
POST TIME, Operation: 8–10, 16
Powell, GEN Colin L.: 2–3, 14–18,
  21, 23–25, 27–35, 45–46, 48–49,

51–53, 57–62, 66–69, 72–74
Price, William: 12, 42
PROMOTE LIBERTY, Operation: 52–53,
  65–67, 74
Quarry Heights, C.Z.: 7, 12, 22,
  24, 33, 35, 48, 65

Radio Nacional broadcasts: 49
Rangers: 22, 25, 34, 37, 39, 67
Rather, Dan: 34
Reactive execution scenario: 20, 24
Reagan, Ronald W.: 6–7, 13–14
RED, Task Force (Rangers): 21–22,
  38–39
Renacer Prison: 22, 40
Reservists call-up: 19, 46, 49, 52–
  53, 66
Rio Hato: 7, 15, 18, 20–22, 31, 34,
  37–40, 42, 51
Ross, Robin: 57
Rules of engagement (ROE): 66

2d Marine Expeditionary Force: 11
6th Marine Expeditionary Brigade: 8
16th Military Police Brigade: 21,
  37, 51
7th Infantry Division (L): 9, 11,
  13, 19, 21, 32, 37, 39, 51, 68
75th Infantry Regiment (Rangers):
  37
Sand Flea exercises: 25
SEAL Teams TWO and FOUR: 23
  (U.S. Navy *Sea-Air-Land* forces)
Security measures, internal: 18–19
SEMPER FI, Task Force (Marines):
  21, 22, 38, 40
Sheafer, RADM Edward D.: 28, 45–46,
  60
Smithsonian hostages: 49, 52
Scowcroft, Lt Gen (USAF, Ret.)
  Brent: 11, 15, 17, 21, 27–29
SOCOM (See U.S. Special Operations
  Command)
Sodano, Cardinal Angelo: 57
Spadafora, Hugo: 6
Special Mission Units: 20
Special operations forces: 2, 7–8,
  17–20, 30, 32, 35, 37–38, 51, 55,

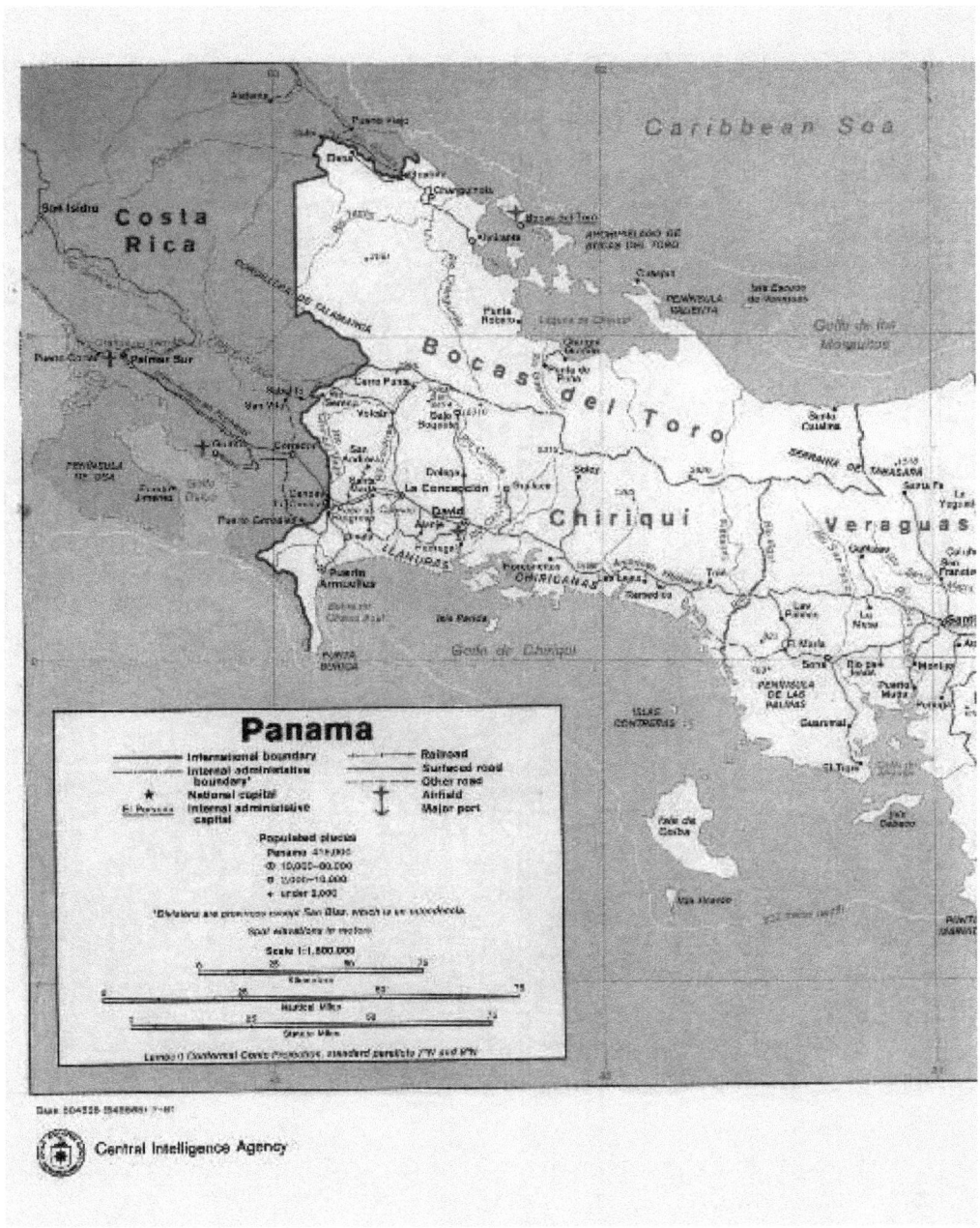

Caribbean Sea

Costa Rica

Bocas del Toro

Chiriquí

Veraguas

CORDILLERA DE TALAMANCA

ARCHIPIÉLAGO DE BOCAS DEL TORO

PENÍNSULA VALIENTE

Golfo de los Mosquitos

SERRANÍA DE TABASARA

Laguna de Chiriquí

PENÍNSULA DE OSA

LLANURAS

CORDILLERA

Golfo de Chiriquí

PENÍNSULA DE LAS PALMAS

ISLAS CONTRERAS

Isla de Coiba

Isla Jicarón

Costa Rica — San Isidro, Puerto Cortés, Palmar Sur, Puerto Jiménez

Panama — Puerto Viejo, Changuinola, Bocas del Toro, Chiriquí Grande, Punta Robalo, Puerto de Pixvae, Santa Catalina, Santa Fe, La Yeguada, Cerro Punta, Volcán, San Andrés, Boquete, Dolega, La Concepción, David, Horconcitos, Puerto Armuelles, Isla Parida, Las Palmas, El María, Soná, Río de Jesús, Guarumal, Montijo, Puerto Mutis, El Tigre

Panama

——	International boundary	
-·-·-	Internal administrative boundary*	
★	National capital	
El Panama	Internal administrative capital	

- ―――― Railroad
- ―――― Surfaced road
- ‑‑‑‑‑ Other road
- + Airfield
- ⚓ Major port

Populated places
Panama 415,000
⊕ 10,000–90,000
⊙ 5,000–10,000
+ under 5,000

*Divisions are provinces except San Blas, which is an intendencia.

Spot elevations in meters

Scale 1:1,800,000

| 0 | 25 | 50 | 75 |
Kilometers

| 0 | 25 | 50 | 75 |
Nautical Miles

| 0 | 25 | 50 | 75 |
Statute Miles

Lambert Conformal Conic Projection, standard parallels 7°N and 9°N

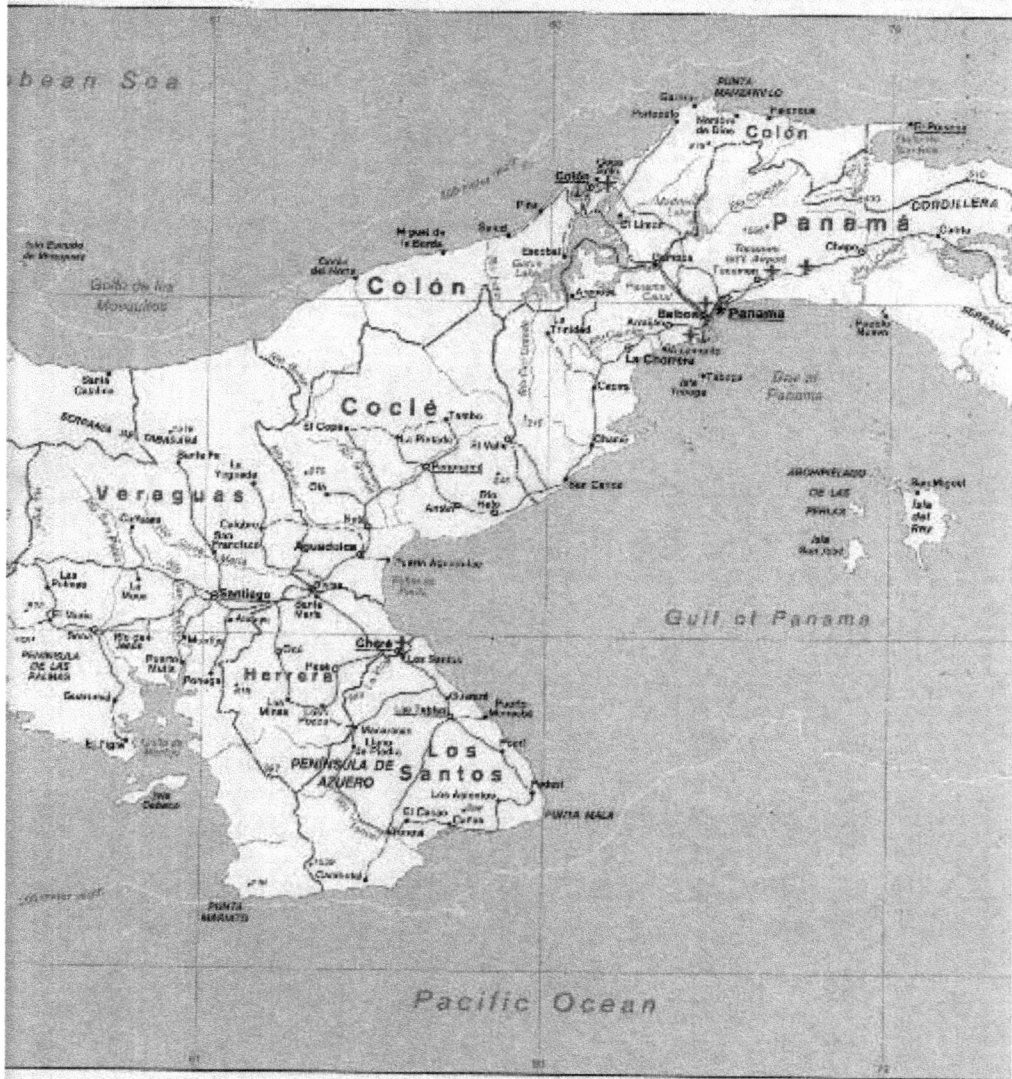

www.ingramcontent.com/pod-product-compliance
Lightning Source LLC
LaVergne TN
LVHW061301060426

835509LV00016B/1668